Contents

Chapter 1   Democracy: legitimacy and the lockdown — from health crisis to democratic crisis?   5

In what ways was the UK's response to the health crisis legitimate? ■ To what extent did the imposition of a lockdown undermine democracy in the UK?

Chapter 2   Pressure groups: the Black Lives Matter movement — methods, influence and success   15

Black Lives Matter: relevance, prominence and influence ■ In what ways were methods associated with the BLM movement criticised?

Chapter 3   Rights in context: civil liberties campaigns in the 2020s   24

Case study 1: Campaigns to support disabled people during the lockdown ■ Case study 2: Challenging facial recognition technology ■ Case study 3: Crowdfunding to widen legal access in the protection of rights

Chapter 4   Political parties in the 2020s: funding, fairness and the future   31

What did the 2019 general election reveal about the state of party funding? ■ Should political parties be funded by the state?

Chapter 5   The influence of the media: is the BBC biased, and does it matter?   37

Why is the influence of the BBC significant? ■ Is the BBC impartial? ■ Case study 1: The BBC and the Dominic Cummings saga, May 2020 ■ Has social media use undermined the integrity of the BBC? ■ Case study 2: Singing at the Proms

Chapter 6   Devolution: the state of the union — stronger than ever, or a dangerous mess?   44

To what extent was the UK's devolved response to the health crisis disjointed? ■ Has the health crisis made Scottish independence more likely? ■ What next for the government of a post-pandemic England?

Annual Update, 2021

Chapter 7 **Parliament:** the House of Lords — too big, too partisan
and time for change?   52

Why was Boris Johnson's dissolution list controversial? ■ Is the
House of Lords too big? ■ Has the House of Lords become too
partisan? ■ Is it time to fully reform the Lords?

Chapter 8 **Parliament and the executive:** the impact of the health
crisis on their relationship   59

The role of backbenchers during the health crisis ■ The work
of select committees ■ The leader of the opposition and prime
minister's questions

Chapter 9 **The prime minister:** how effective was Boris Johnson in
controlling the health crisis?   65

In what ways was the prime minister effective in dictating
events during the health crisis? ■ In what ways did the prime
minister fail to control events effectively?

ANNUAL UPDATE 2021

UK POLITICS

Nick Gallop

HODDER
EDUCATION
AN HACHETTE UK COMPANY

Acknowledgements

Every effort has been made to trace all copyright holders, but if any have been inadvertently overlooked, the Publishers will be pleased to make the necessary arrangements at the first opportunity.

Although every effort has been made to ensure that website addresses are correct at time of going to press, Hodder Education cannot be held responsible for the content of any website mentioned in this book. It is sometimes possible to find a relocated web page by typing in the address of the home page for a website in the URL window of your browser.

Hachette UK's policy is to use papers that are natural, renewable and recyclable products and made from wood grown in well-managed forests and other controlled sources. The logging and manufacturing processes are expected to conform to the environmental regulations of the country of origin.

Orders: please contact Hachette UK Distribution, Hely Hutchinson Centre, Milton Road, Didcot, Oxfordshire, OX11 7HH. Telephone: +44 (0)1235 827827. E-mail education@hachette.co.uk. Lines are open from 9 a.m. to 5 p.m., Monday to Friday. You can also order through our website: www.hoddereducation.co.uk.

ISBN: 978 1 3983 2694 1

First published in 2021 by

Hodder Education,
An Hachette UK Company
Carmelite House
50 Victoria Embankment
London EC4Y 0DZ

www.hoddereducation.co.uk

Impression number 10 9 8 7 6 5 4 3 2 1

Year 2025 2024 2023 2022 2021

Cover photo © Joao — stock.adobe.com

Typeset by Integra Software Services Pvt. Ltd, Pondicherry, India

Printed by CPI Group (UK) Ltd, Croydon, CR0 4YY

A catalogue record for this title is available from the British Library.

Chapter 1

Democracy: legitimacy and the lockdown — from health crisis to democratic crisis?

Focus

The nature of democracy features in all examination specifications. Students need to analyse and evaluate the similarities and differences and advantages and disadvantages of direct and representative democracy. For longer responses, students are likely to need a strong understanding of the contested nature of democracy in the UK. As well as the extent to which there is a participation crisis, a democratic deficit and a case for democratic reform, the question of legitimacy — the rightful use of government power — is an essential feature of analysis of democracy in the UK.

Edexcel	UK Politics 1.1	Features of representative democracy and direct democracy; similarities and differences; advantages and disadvantages and the case for reform
AQA	3.1.2.1	Analysing direct and representative democracy and evaluating the nature of democracy in the UK

Context

The lockdown in 2020 represented a multi-dimensional challenge to democracy in the UK. On 23 March 2020, the prime minister was unequivocal in his instruction to UK citizens: 'We are giving one simple instruction — you must stay at home.' A fortnight later, the health secretary reiterated that people must 'stay in their homes' over Easter in a 'test of the nation's resolve'.

The legislation that provided the basis for these extraordinary directives was the Coronavirus Act 2020. Fast-tracked through Parliament in just 4 sitting days, the Act provided public bodies with emergency powers to respond to the Covid-19 pandemic. It contained wide-ranging provisions to contain and slow the spread of the virus, to ease the burden on frontline health services, to provide unprecedented levels of economic support, to delay elections and to substantially alter the way that Parliament functioned.

The UK's response to the health crisis presented some profound democratic challenges, leaving barely any aspect of political life untouched and generating issues that will be debated for years. These include:

- Even in liberal democracies, state-of-emergency measures are sometimes required to combat threats such as war or natural disasters. However, any extension to state power should be strictly defined and proportionate to the scale of the crisis. In what ways was the UK's response to the health crisis legitimate?

■ A delicate balance exists between liberty and security within liberal democracies, centring upon how much freedom citizens are prepared to give up in order for society to function effectively. To what extent did the imposition of a lockdown undermine democracy in the UK?

Box 1.1 Key definitions

Legitimacy: a political principle claimed by governments that succeed in winning a mandate following victory in democratic elections. In addition to this, government decisions and actions need to be considered 'rightful' to retain legitimacy and they should enjoy broad support.

Lockdown: in the context of the health crisis, the confinement of people to their homes in order to reduce risks to themselves and others.

In what ways was the UK's response to the health crisis legitimate?

The earliest information on the threat posed by the Covid-19 virus indicated that it was more infectious than other coronaviruses (such as SARS or MERS-CoV) but potentially less deadly. However, in the absence of effective treatment or vaccines, the risk to people with underlying health conditions was serious.

In the wake of Covid-19's rapid and initially almost unnoticed global spread in early 2020, lockdown measures began to be enforced in many countries to bring overall transmission rates down and to try to spread infections over a longer timeframe to ensure that health services were not overwhelmed.

For lockdowns to have the desired effect, measures need to be strict and are likely to affect many aspects of daily life for a prolonged period of time. With that in mind, ways in which the introduction of lockdown measures in the UK could be considered legitimate are outlined below.

The UK was one of the last states to impose a lockdown

In early 2020, almost all major global states enforced a lockdown similar to the UK's, although the UK was among the last in Europe to do so. The majority of larger European states, including the UK, had detected their first cases by early February 2020. While transmission rates are difficult to compare, as testing varied widely from one state to another, Italy imposed a lockdown 2 weeks earlier than the UK, with Spain and France a week before. The UK's national lockdown commenced on 23 March 2020.

Even as the spread of the Covid-19 virus reached the proportions of a global pandemic, the UK prime minister's reluctance to introduce strict measures was widely noted. Boris Johnson spent much of his career as journalist, writer and politician condemning ideas of the 'nanny state', critical of government policies that curtail individual liberties. Johnson's personal brand of Conservatism is one which stresses that people should be free to live their lives how they wish with minimal state interference.

There was widespread support for the lockdown and continued observance of it

An important element of legitimate government action is that it should enjoy broad support, accepted despite potentially being disagreed with. Two weeks after the imposition of the lockdown there remained extensive public support for measures to control the spread of the virus. According to an Ipsos MORI poll in the early days of April 2020, 89% of respondents said that they strongly supported (68%) or tended to support (21%) the measures.

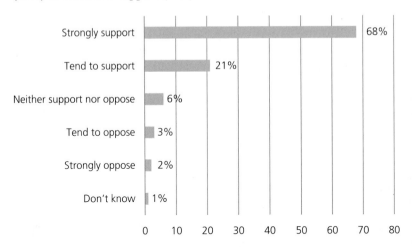

Figure 1.1 Public support for the lockdown and perceptions of the risk of coronavirus

Adapted from Ipsos MORI, 16 April 2020

The survey also revealed that just 14% of respondents agreed that 'too much fuss' was being made about the risk, contrasting with responses to the same question during the swine flu pandemic of 2009 when 55% agreed that there was 'too much fuss'.

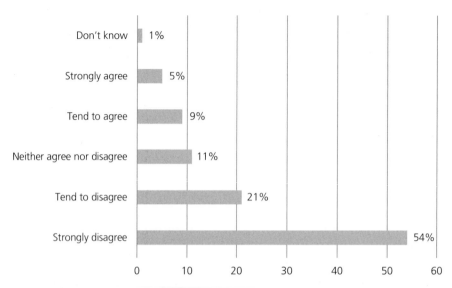

Figure 1.2 Responses to the question 'Do you agree or disagree that too much fuss is being made about the risk of coronavirus?'

Adapted from Ipsos MORI, 16 April 2020

Measures were seen as proportionate to the threat

The rightful use of government power is the basis of legitimacy. In this regard, the UK's lockdown was similar to those of many other states, and less extreme than some. In the UK, responsibility for healthcare is devolved to the regions. The lockdown measures imposed and relaxed within the four nations in the UK differed a little but were broadly similar to each other (see Chapter 6). And while limitations on movement and temporary closures of commercial and retail businesses (except those providing essential services) characterised virtually all lockdowns globally, some states were considerably stricter than the UK. These included:

- France — where citizens were required to keep a record of when they left their homes and faced much stricter requirements to remain 'within a distance of one kilometre maximum of your home, for one hour'.
- Spain — where going out for exercise was not allowed except to walk the dog, but only around the block. Parents were not allowed to take children out unless they had to shop and were not permitted to leave children alone at home.
- Jordan — where leaving home for anything other than strictly defined reasons was punishable by up to 1 year in jail. At the time that the UK imposed its lockdown, Jordan had arrested and detained over 800 people for lockdown breaches.

Emergency powers included appropriate checks and balances

Although the coronavirus legislation was fast-tracked through Parliament in just 4 sitting days, it contained a range of checks and balances that limited the emergency powers granted to the government. Under the Coronavirus Act 2020:

- Emergency measures to tackle the coronavirus were time-limited to 2 years and not all measures were to be used immediately.

- While directions made by ministers relating to potentially infectious people and to limit events and gatherings did not need to be put before Parliament, any other measures had to be taken by statutory instrument which requires parliamentary approval. For example, on 4 November 2020 MPs voted on the introduction of a short national lockdown for England.
- The Act required the secretary of state for health to publish a report every 2 months on the use of non-devolved powers of the Act.
- The Act stipulated that parliamentary debates must be held in both Houses of Parliament 1 year after the bill became law.
- MPs would have an opportunity to formally debate the continued operation of the Act's temporary provisions every 6 months, and on 30 September 2020, MPs voted overwhelmingly in favour of the motion to renew the temporary provisions of the Coronavirus Act.

Box 1.3   What are emergency powers?

Emergency powers refer to the government's ability to respond rapidly to public emergencies by introducing measures that may affect fundamental rights, such as the right to liberty. Emergency powers in the context of the Covid-19 health crisis are underpinned by previous legislation, particularly the Public Health (Control of Disease) Act 1984 and the Civil Contingencies Act 2004. Emergency powers permit the government, within legal limits, to make regulations without an Act of Parliament and to take actions it would not normally be permitted to take.

Adapted from the Institute for Government, www.instituteforgovernment.org.uk

The government attempted to make itself accountable during the lockdown

Ministers kept people directly informed during the lockdown with daily briefings under media scrutiny. The daily Downing Street coronavirus briefings lasted for more than 3 months and the broadcasts were watched by millions at home. Ministers and scientists were routinely quizzed on the many problems and shortcomings of the government's response to the pandemic, such as the supply of protective equipment, testing and the UK's significant death toll.

The levels of public engagement with the daily briefings remained high with a daily average of 4 million viewers. In addition to the daily briefings, over 25 million viewers watched the two major national addresses made by the prime minister — the first on 23 March 2020 to announce lockdown measures and the second on 10 May 2020 to announce measures being eased. Downing Street briefings and news conferences resumed from 5 November 2020 during the second period of national lockdown.

However, in late April 2020, a poll by *Press Gazette* — which campaigns for ethical journalism — found that 70% of respondents to its poll did not think the press was doing an effective job of holding the government to account.

Box 1.4 **Poll: journalists 'not doing good job' during daily Covid-19 briefings**

A total of 1,020 people responded to the question: 'Do you think journalists have done a good job of holding the Government to account during the daily UK Covid-19 press briefings?' which ran on *Press Gazette* for 1 week. In response, 718 said 'no' (70%), while 302 said 'yes' (30%).

In recent weeks, journalists have been the sole real opposition to the government after Parliament shut down for a month having voted through lockdown measures to curb the spread of coronavirus. At the same time the Labour Party was going through the process of electing a new leader, while the Liberal Democrats remain leaderless after Jo Swinson lost her seat at the last general election.

www.pressgazette.co.uk, 22 April 2020

To what extent did the imposition of a lockdown undermine democracy in the UK?

There are notable recent examples of authoritarian leaders using crises — real or perceived — to further anti-democratic ends. Indeed many leaders, such as Viktor Orbán in Hungary, Hugo Chávez in Venezuela and Recep Tayyip Erdoğan in Turkey, have done so while enjoying sustained levels of popular support.

Such 'anti-democratic ends' often relate to extensions of executive power, censorship of the press, manipulation of the judicial process, and the delaying or undermining of elections.

Box 1.5 **The health crisis and global 'power grabs'**

- In March 2020, Hungary's prime minister Viktor Orbán used his party's majority in parliament to extend the country's 'state of danger' with the power to rule by decree indefinitely. Although members of parliament voted unanimously to end rule by decree later, in June 2020, many opposition groups argued that the Orbán administration had greatly expanded its powers during the crisis.
- In Turkey it was claimed that President Erdoğan used the health crisis to increase control of social media companies with new executive powers hidden within legislation that dealt mainly with economic measures. Hundreds were subsequently arrested in Turkey for 'provocative posts' about the health crisis on social media.

While the necessity of a lockdown to lower the rate of transmission of the virus appears to have been supported by a majority of people in the UK, from a political point of view it nevertheless had a severe impact on liberty, rights and the proper functioning of the UK's democratic institutions and political systems.

On a philosophical level, the delicate balance between liberty and security — the extent to which citizens are prepared to give up their liberty for the protection of the state and for the proper functioning of society — has preoccupied political thinkers such as Thomas Hobbes and John Locke for centuries. Needless to say, the lockdown upset this balance on a dramatic scale.

On a practical level, some commentators argued at the time that the lockdown 'cure' could well turn out to be far worse than the original disease.

Box 1.6 **History may judge the lockdown to be a monumental mistake**

The longer we remain in the limbo of lockdown the more we are harming the world's economies, healthcare provision, our mental health and our children's education. When the reckoning comes we may well find that the cure turned out to be far worse than the disease, devastating though the disease undoubtedly is. I fear that history will judge the lockdown as a monumental mistake on a truly global scale.

Mark Woolhouse (a member of the Scottish Government Covid-19 Advisory Group), *New Statesman*, 3 July 2020

In this regard, as others, the health crisis in the UK resulted in several developments that undermined democracy.

Freedom of movement was severely curtailed

Key thinker John Stuart Mill asserted that individuals should be free to live their lives according to how they wish, as long as their actions do not harm others. However, the government's response to the health crisis saw many fundamental *individual* freedoms — ones formerly taken for granted such as the freedom of movement, of association and assembly — severely restricted in order to protect *collective* health. For many, this was an unacceptable price to pay.

Coronavirus legislation lacked appropriate constraints

The British Institute of Human Rights (**www.bihr.org.uk**) was critical of the legislation that supported the emergency measures. Notwithstanding the 'legitimate public health goals', the BIHR highlighted a number of provisions that in its view undermined the UK's commitment to appropriate democratic oversight. Of particular note to the BIHR was that the emergency powers, that had such a significantly adverse impact on many, were enabled for up to 2 years. The Act required Parliament to review and grant its extension every 6 months. When the first parliamentary review occurred on 30 September 2020, many MPs were angered about the 90-minute limit for discussion, including Conservative MP Sir Charles Walker who branded it an 'utter, utter disgrace'. The motion to extend the Act was voted for by 330 MPs, with 24 against.

Box 1.7 **A 2-year timeframe for extended government powers**

Other legislation allowing emergency powers, such as the Civil Contingencies Act 2004, contains clauses which mean that these powers lapse after 30 days. A 6-month parliamentary review can only be triggered if there is support for the whole Act to expire. This means that if there are concerns about any one section of the Act, they must review the continuation of the whole Act.

Source: adapted from **www.bihr.org.uk** under 'Concerns with provisions of the Coronavirus Bill'

Normal democratic processes were suspended or delayed

Almost all aspects of the functioning of the state were affected by the lockdown, including the judicial process and cabinet decision making. Some of the most notable effects were to parliamentary scrutiny and the delaying of elections:

- **Parliamentary scrutiny:** for several weeks in March and April 2020 the UK Parliament ceased to function. During that time police were granted powers to fine or arrest those who broke lockdown rules and there was a failure to supply adequate protective equipment to healthcare workers and an inability to test in sufficient quantities. Yet parliamentary scrutiny of the government's response to the health crisis was undermined by ineffectual online technology that saw the digital reopening of democratic institutions take several weeks.
- **Delayed elections:** on 7 May 2020 a raft of elections were due to take place. These included elections for 118 English councils and the Greater London Assembly, and for 8 city or combined authority mayors including the Mayor of London. While elections have been delayed before, notably during the First and Second World Wars and briefly prior to the 2001 general election due to the foot and mouth crisis, their postponement for a year was far longer than recommended by the Electoral Commission.

Police powers were greatly enhanced

The legislation granted the police extensive powers to enforce the lockdown. The police had the power to fine people who were in breach of specific lockdown measures, to take 'such action as is necessary' in order to disperse gatherings of more than two people (other than members of the same household), and to compel individuals outside their homes without 'reasonable excuse' to return to their homes.

However, there was widespread criticism of the lack of clarity in the regulations and particular confusion over what behaviour had become 'illegal' (therefore against the law of the land and enforceable by the police) and what was merely contrary to government guidance.

> **Box 1.8** **Heavy-handed police are enforcing restrictions that do not exist in law**
>
> The coronavirus regulations do not limit us to one form of exercise a day or define Easter eggs as non-essential. Daily government advice on the Covid-19 lockdown routinely overstates the extent of restrictions on movement. Misconceptions about them are now firmly embedded in the national and police consciousness. We have recently seen wrongful convictions under the Coronavirus Act, which applies only to those suspected of carrying the infection, and excessive and erroneous 'enforcement' of children playing in their own front garden and of a young man cuffed for helping his mother. Drones fly over parks, the Peak District and even back gardens. One chief constable tweeted that he might soon be directing his officers to rifle through shopping trolleys to check items.
>
> Chris Henley QC, *The Times*, 16 April 2020

The case for the UK's lockdown may take years to establish

While there was broad support for the introduction of lockdown measures, it would be wrong to suggest that there was anything approaching a consensus — either on the scientific modelling to validate the measures, or the relative balance between health and economic priorities. In addition, acquiring the data to make meaningful comparisons between different countries, ones adopting different approaches to containing the virus, may take many years or never be fully possible.

However, some early indicators suggested that while early lockdowns appeared to have been successful in slowing transmission rates, many countries followed similar patterns out of lockdown, with infection rates rapidly reaching pre-lockdown levels and little appetite for reinstating previous measures. In addition, several factors and developments in the spread of the virus appeared confusing and contradictory, including:

- From the summer months onwards, statistics in the UK travelled in different directions. The number of daily infections rose steadily into the tens of thousands, yet the death toll remained substantially lower than the spring 'peak'. The true level of cases in early 2020 and improved hospital treatment later in the year were largely behind this.
- At the peak of testing, the UK was regularly conducting around 350,000 daily tests. By mid-November 2020, some 35 million tests had been processed — more than double that of France. Such disparities between countries in the number of tests processed, and the growing targeting of testing in areas of the UK that saw rises in cases, made comparisons between countries complicated and unhelpful.
- As the lockdown eased in June, congested beaches and protest marches were sources of widespread alarm. Yet infection data in the weeks that followed suggested that they made little impact on the overall spread of the virus. On the other hand, the return to university campuses in September 2020 saw dramatic increases in the transmission of the virus, yet the return to schools did not.
- One of the main objectives of the lockdown was to ensure that the National Health Service was not overwhelmed. In reality, health officials revealed that there were far more empty beds in hospitals than usual over the summer months, yet the repurposing of the NHS had led to growing waiting lists for many life-threatening illnesses.

Connections and comparisons

- There are a substantial number of cross-topic links, not least in terms of the divergent 'four nations approach' adopted within the UK. As discussed further in Chapter 6, healthcare responsibilities are devolved to the nations, leading to differing approaches in the regions. While such divergence could be considered advantageous in targeting approaches to tackling localised issues, the incoherence of the UK's overall approach was more often the source of conflict and confusion.
- The relationship between liberty and security — in this case the extent to which the severe restrictions of the lockdown were necessary — is an important element of the social contract theory advanced by key thinkers Thomas Hobbes and John Locke and further developed by Jean-Jacques Rousseau in his *Social Contract* (1762). Professor Lea Ypi of the London School of Economics noted that 'if the state has emerged from the pandemic as a more prominent force in our public life, the idea of popular sovereignty that serves to legitimise it — the notion that we are equal authors of the laws we are required to obey — has never been weaker' (*New Statesman*, July 2020). The only way that the authority of the state can be justified is through appropriate democratic processes. For Rousseau as for others, the role of the state is not one of domination and supremacy but emancipation and of the facilitation of freedom.

Exam success

Students tackling examination questions on this topic will need to place the issues associated with the UK's response to the health crisis in context with wider debates about democracy in the UK. Longer responses that require effective links to be made between contemporary events and examination specifications may be framed as follows:

- Evaluate the extent to which the UK's democracy is legitimate. (Edexcel-style, 30 marks)
- 'The nature of democracy in the UK is legitimate.' Analyse and evaluate this statement. (AQA-style, 25 marks)

Well before recent events, concerns with the legitimacy of the UK's democratic institutions and processes focused upon constitutional arrangements that lack clarity and precision, devolved arrangements that are uncertain, an unelected legislative body in the form of the House of Lords, unrepresentative electoral outcomes, declining levels of political participation, and concerns about the developing role of the judiciary and the protection of rights.

What next?

Watch: 'RSM In Conversation Live with Lord Jonathan Sumption', YouTube, 16 July 2020.

Read: Open Democracy's 'What's your vision for the world after coronavirus?', which can be found at **www.opendemocracy.net/en/world-after-covid**

Read: 'Legitimacy and the lockdown' by Nick Gallop in *Politics Review*, Volume 30, Issue 3, February 2021

Chapter 2

Pressure groups: the Black Lives Matter movement — methods, influence and success

Focus

Students require an effective understanding of how pressure groups exert influence on the political process and how and why their methods differ depending on their aims. Students also need to evaluate why some groups are more successful than others, and how some groups may be adjudged to undermine democracy — potentially by using unconstitutional or illegal tactics to achieve their aims — while others are considered to support it, often by furthering social justice, raising awareness or enhancing engagement.

Edexcel	UK Politics 1.3	How different pressure groups exert influence and how their methods vary in contemporary politics
AQA	3.1.2.4	Methods used by pressure groups

Context

The death of George Floyd in the USA on 25 May 2020, its timing and cruelty, with widely shared film footage of him pleading for his life as a police officer knelt on his neck, provoked a level of international outrage that convulsed many countries around the world. It led to sustained protests and demonstrations about the continuing presence of racism, prejudice and discrimination in society.

A significant consequence of the killing was that the Black Lives Matter (BLM) movement, already widely known in the USA, came to much greater public prominence in the UK over the summer of 2020. The aims of the movement in the UK are to highlight the ill-effects and suffering caused by entrenched prejudice. As explained on BLM's UK website, they are to 'dismantle systemic racism, systematic racial discrimination and social and criminal injustices to create fairer and just systems where all people are equal'.

The subject matter is emotive and challenging, and continues to provoke discussion nationally, as well as politically. Furthermore, the methods, influence and controversies associated with the BLM movement provide invaluable contemporary evidence for students of politics to support understanding and evaluation of the complex politics of protest movements, especially set against contested interpretations of British history.

> ### Box 2.1 Key definition
>
> **Black Lives Matter (BLM):** a decentralised political and social movement promoting non-violent civil disobedience to protest against police brutality against black people and to promote an end to racial discrimination. Beginning in the USA in 2013 with the hashtag #BlackLivesMatter, protests spread to the UK in 2016, increasingly reaching the mainstream in the wake of events like the Grenfell fire and the Windrush scandal.

Black Lives Matter: relevance, prominence and influence

There are a number of interrelated factors which help to explain the context of the BLM protests for racial justice that occurred in the UK in 2020, and the factors supporting the movement's relevance and influence. Sparked by a police killing 4,000 miles away that generated sustained demonstration and violence in the USA (see Table 2.1), the influence of BLM protests in the UK in 2020 centred on substantially raised awareness of racial discrimination, popularising debates about Britain's past and building coalitions to pressure for political change.

Table 2.1 A timeline of UK-based events following
the death of George Floyd in the USA

Date	Details
25 May 2020	George Floyd was killed while under arrest and in police custody in Minneapolis. Widely circulated film of events leading up to his death showed a police officer kneeling on Floyd's neck while the suspect pleaded 'Please, I can't breathe'.
26 May 2020	Within 24 hours of Floyd's death, residents of Minneapolis had taken to the streets to demand justice and raise awareness of the case. Protests and marches centred on the city's police precinct, amid calls to 'defund the police', and were soon followed in other US cities.
27 May 2020	Within 48 hours of the death, following concerted pressure from the Minneapolis Black Lives Matter (BLM) protestors, all four officers involved in the incident were fired, while police officer Derek Chauvin who knelt on Floyd's neck was charged with third degree murder and an FBI investigation was launched.
28 May 2020	With marches and demonstrations spreading across the USA, the first UK protest took place when around 20 participants held banners supporting the BLM movement outside the US Embassy in London.
6 June 2020	In the days that followed, demonstrations took place in several cities across the UK. On Saturday 6 June, many thousands of people demonstrated in London outside Downing Street and along Whitehall in what was to be the largest single UK protest of the summer. Clashes with police led to 23 officers receiving treatment for injuries and 14 arrests.

Date	Details
7 June 2020	Protests continuing across the UK included a number of widely circulated incidents. In London amid clashes with police, protestors defaced the Cenotaph and a statue of Winston Churchill. In Bristol a statue of the 17th-century slave trader Edward Colston was toppled and defaced.
13 June 2020	Mainly peaceful BLM protests continued across the UK, several of them attracting counter-protests. An official BLM protest planned for 13 June was cancelled following concerns that far-right activists planned to disrupt it. Counter-demonstrations saw protestors gather around statue sites across the UK, many of them resulting in violence, clashes with police, injuries and arrests.
21 June 2020	Following further BLM-organised protests across the UK, the final largescale event of the summer took place in Leeds.

Raising awareness of systemic discrimination within the UK's criminal justice system

There is little doubt that the particularly shocking film footage of events leading up to the death of George Floyd played a major part in rapid global engagement with the case and the mobilisation of many thousands worldwide in protest against the killing. While similar levels of police brutality in the UK are mercifully rare, official statistics quoted by the BBC in 2020 nevertheless showed that police in England and Wales are still 'three times more likely to arrest a black person than a white person and five times more likely to use force'.

Similarly, while the scale of deaths in police custody is dramatically different to that of the USA, black people in the UK are still more than twice as likely to die in police custody than white people, according to a recent report into police conduct compiled by the Independent Office for Police Conduct (IOPC).

Box 2.2 **'Systemic racism and police brutality are British problems too'**

Though the numbers of deaths following police contact are thankfully not as bad in the UK as in the USA, we should be anything but complacent when it comes to our own structural problems with racism or policing. Institutional racism exists at every level of our criminal justice system, from who gets stopped and searched, to who gets arrested, to who gets charged, to who gets convicted.

Source: Kojo Koram, 'Systemic racism and police brutality are British problems too', *The Guardian*, 4 June 2020

Receiving renewed attention in 2020 was the Lammy Review, an examination of Criminal Justice System statistics commissioned by former prime minister David Cameron and delivered by Labour MP David Lammy in 2017. Among other findings, the Review revealed that the proportion of black people in England and

Wales in prison is higher in relation to their share of the general population than the corresponding figure in the US. Figures are starker still when considering younger inmates specifically, as 48% of under-18s in custody are from black or other ethnic minority backgrounds.

Box 2.3 **'Greater disproportionality than the USA'**

Despite making up just 14% of the population, BAME men and women make up 25% of prisoners, while over 40% of young people in custody are from BAME backgrounds. If our prison population reflected the make-up of England and Wales, we would have over 9,000 fewer people in prison — the equivalent of 12 average-sized prisons. There is greater disproportionality in the number of Black people in prisons here than in the United States.

Source: the Lammy Review, www.tinyurl.com/yyctz8zf

Contrary to criticism that protesters were 'jumping on an American bandwagon' to protest about a police issue highly specific to the USA, the BLM movement in the UK renewed engagement with and dialogue about criminal justice system statistics that highlighted evidence of deep-rooted discrimination.

Popularising debates about Britain's past

For many, the toppling of the statue of former slave trader and philanthropist Edward Colston in Bristol in June 2020 was both symbolic of the 'toxicity' at the heart of British history and long overdue. Standing as it did as a defining symbol of 'white supremacy', the case for the removal of this 'affront' had seen growing support.

For others, it was a misdirected and unsupportable reaction. It was an act condemned as 'utterly disgraceful' by Home Secretary Priti Patel, and 'completely wrong' by Labour leader Keir Starmer. For those appalled by the criminal damage, it was further evidence of a 'culture war' being waged over Britain's past that had left the country polarised and incensed.

Box 2.4 **Reactions to the toppling of the statue of Edward Colston**

I can't and won't pretend the statue of a slave trader in a city I was born and grew up in wasn't an affront to me and people like me. People in Bristol who don't want that statue in the middle of the city came together and it is my job to unite, hear those voices and hold those truths together for people for who that statue is a personal affront.

Marvin Rees, Mayor of Bristol, 8 June 2020

People can campaign for the removal of a statue but what happened yesterday was a criminal act and when the criminal law is broken that is unacceptable and the police will want to hold to account those responsible. The PM absolutely understands the strength of feeling, but in this country, we settle our differences democratically and if people wanted the removal of the statue there are democratic routes which can be followed.

Official spokesman for the prime minister, 8 June 2020

Whichever perspective holds sway, the pathway towards the toppling of Edward Colston's statue is to be seen in context — both local and national. Locally, many towns and cities have been involved in spirited civic debate for many years about how and whether to accommodate or eliminate benefactors whose wealth was based on slave labour. Nationally, the act should be seen as a small part of a lengthy and ongoing process of grappling with a contested past. A past that for many people does not stand up well to modern-day scrutiny.

However, while this grappling process may well be going on the world over — from Belgium to South Africa, and from America's former confederate states to Australia — for many, the BLM movement in the UK succeeded in shifting the debate about Britain's colonial past from the confines of localised discussion and debate into the broad daylight of the political mainstream and onto Britain's streets.

Building a coalition to challenge inequality and prejudice

For many, the BLM movement gave full and sustained opposing voice to a deeply entrenched and deadly culture of discrimination and prejudice in the UK. Official statistics show that in recent years and compared to white people:

- Black people are more than ten times as likely to be stopped and searched by the police (source: Ethnicity facts and figures at gov.uk)
- Black people are more than twice as likely to face unemployment (source: Office for National Statistics)
- Black mothers are more than five times as likely to die in pregnancy than white mothers (source: UK Confidential Enquiry into Maternal Deaths).
- Black people have a lower life expectancy because more of them live in areas of deprivation compared to the general population (source: Public Health Outcomes Framework: Health Equity Report)

From its roots in the UK in 2016, the BLM movement has travelled far and fast in building relevance and influence. It has turned a US-based movement protesting primarily about police brutality into a UK-based one that has highlighted and exposed many forms of injustice and discrimination based upon race. Its founder Patrick Vernon identifies several traumatic recent events in the wake of which the movement has sought to bring affected people together to press for recognition and lasting change:

- In 2017 the Grenfell Tower fire killed 72 people, 57 of whom were from ethnic minority backgrounds. Leslie Thomas QC, representing bereaved families in the 2020 inquiry, said the fire was 'inextricably linked with race'.
- In 2018 the Windrush scandal saw many thousands of British residents from former Commonwealth countries incorrectly informed that their status was illegal. Some of them lost their homes, their employment and were forcibly deported.
- In 2020, the health crisis shed further light on the social and economic difficulties faced by many ethnic minority communities. Poverty, over-crowded housing and low-waged employment were all highlighted as factors in explaining far higher death rates among ethnic minorities, with black people more than twice as likely to die with Covid-19 than white people.

For campaigners like Patrick Vernon, running through these examples is the common thread of official neglect and indifference stemming from entrenched racism. The BLM movement has sought to provide a platform to force sustained recognition and full acknowledgment of these issues.

> ### Box 2.5   Black communities speaking out
>
> It raises that vexed question, are we British? Are we really British? Are we valued? Is our contribution valued in this country? The whole Black Lives Matter thing crystallises that. They want to take action because the current democratic process is not working for people.
>
> Source: Patrick Vernon talking to the BBC: https://www.bbc.co.uk/news/uk-52997848

In what ways were methods associated with the BLM movement criticised?

While the continuing corrosive presence of racism in society remains abhorrent, some methods associated with the BLM movement have drawn criticism. In particular, undemocratic tactics, such as civil disobedience or criminal damage, and a lack of civility, such as anonymous online harassment and threats, have been highlighted as counter-productive to a movement that seeks to challenge injustice, intimidation and fear.

Callout culture: accountability or score-settling?

Versions of callout culture have existed for as long as humans have lived together, utilised by the marginalised and the dispossessed to highlight injustice and to push for change and betterment. The use of social media to 'call out' prejudice and discrimination is a significant recent feature of several prominent social movements such as #Metoo and BLM.

Supporters of callout culture see a process that enables those who would not otherwise have had a voice to expose wrongdoing and injustice. Indeed for some alleged transgressors, retribution via callout can be swift and painful. In 2020, 500 gyms dropped their affiliation with fitness company CrossFit after its founder was called out on social media for 'trivialising the concerns of Black Lives Matter'.

> ### Box 2.6   Apologies, action plans, and resignation announcements
>
> Twitter has exploded with stories from people of colour about pay disparities, discrimination, and offensive speech in their workplaces. It has also been a place where historical instances of insensitivity by companies and entertainers have been put on blast. The results of such outcries have been swift and concrete, with many brands, celebs, and CEOs issuing apologies, action plans, and resignation announcements.
>
> Source: Spencer Kornhaber, 'It's not callout culture, it's accountability', The Atlantic, 16 June 2020

However, although broadly supportive of the power of callout culture to reinforce the BLM protests on the streets, even the likes of *Atlantic* writer Spencer Kornhaber recognise that many callouts bear 'all the hallmarks of Twitter excess: the personal score-settling, the juicy attention-grabbing details, the focus on celebrity'.

Others such as celebrated African-American academic, feminist and activist Loretta Ross emphasise that some callouts may be justified 'to challenge provocateurs who deliberately hurt others, or for powerful people beyond our reach' but argues that 'most public shaming is horizontal and done by those who believe they have greater integrity or more sophisticated analyses. They become the self-appointed guardians of political purity'.

> ### Box 2.7   A courtroom composed of clicks
>
> Callouts are often louder and more vicious on the internet, amplified by the 'clicktivist' culture that provides anonymity for awful behaviour. I wonder if contemporary social movements have absorbed the most useful lessons from the past about how to hold each other accountable while doing extremely difficult and risky social justice work. Can we avoid individualising oppression and not use the movement as our personal therapy space?
>
> Source: Loretta Ross, 'I'm a Black feminist. I think call-out culture is toxic', *New York Times*, August 2019

Similarly, former US president Barack Obama has recently rebuked the self-indulgence of callout culture. Obama challenged young activists who rush to judge others on social media by explaining that callouts 'can give the illusion that you're effecting change, even if that is not true'. For Obama, the short-term satisfaction of shaming another — of 'tweeting a hashtag about how you didn't do something right or used the wrong word' — is rarely followed by long-term change.

Other controversies and debates include perspectives on the broader BLM agenda and the methods employed:

- **Re-racialising society:** Alexander Pelling-Bruce writing in *The Spectator* (July 2020) noted the 'pernicious fallacy that we are best understood through the prism of race and culture' — something that, he argues, preserves and perpetuates division upon racial grounds. Of particular concern to the likes of Pelling-Bruce is the self-serving opportunity that the BLM movement has provided for white people to ostentatiously acknowledge their 'sin of whiteness' and 'elevate themselves above their supposedly parochial fellow citizens'.
- **Decolonising the curriculum:** anti-racist campaigners have long called for the reconstruction of an educational curriculum which, they argue, propagates both the UK's colonial legacy and white, western superiority. For example, black history within the school curriculum, according to research by *The Guardian*, is almost exclusively framed around slavery, colonialism and victimhood, rather than black British history, black culture and migration. However, many warn against the possibility of curriculum capture: 'Rather than simply endorsing complaints from the most vocal students and staff,'

argues Steven Greer in the *Times Higher Education* (July 2020), 'we must react rigorously to curricular exclusions of all kinds.'

- **Criticising aspects of the BLM agenda:** for some, a lack of fulsome support for the BLM agenda proved costly and resulted in further division. Examples include Nick Buckley, the award-winning chief executive of Mancunian Way, a charity that he founded to support disadvantaged young people in Manchester for nearly a decade. In June 2020 Buckley drew attention to the 'far-left agenda' of BLM UK on a blog. When faced with a petition of 465 signatories accusing Buckley of 'insensitive' and 'inappropriate' comments, the charity's four trustees dismissed the founding chief executive. Within days, a counter-petition for Buckley's reinstatement had amassed 17,500 signatures. The original trustees resigned, and Buckley was reinstated.

Connections and comparisons

- In the USA, the killing of a black person by a police officer is sadly far from uncommon, with reliable estimates putting the rate at more than one every other day. In a country where black males aged between 15 and 24 make up just 2% of the population, they represent over 15% of police-related deaths. The issue is so incendiary that BLM campaigns in the USA, such as #WhatMatters2020, served to unite the power of the black vote ahead of the 2020 presidential election by drawing attention to issues of racial injustice.
- Heightened sensitivity towards statuary and other forms of lasting public recognition is far from unique as a British concern. In 2020, Mahatma Gandhi, the Indian independence leader famed for his philosophy of non-violence, was tipped to be on the face of a new coin issued by the Royal Mint. An unexpected public discussion ensued which drew attention to Gandhi's well-documented racism towards black Africans, evident during his time as a young lawyer in South Africa. Indeed a Gandhi statue, found to be particularly offensive to many black Africans, has already been removed from a university campus in Ghana.

Exam success

Longer examination questions which relate to this topic are likely to focus on the extent to which pressure groups support or undermine democracy. While the rise of social media has clearly improved engagement and participation and enhanced the UK's pluralist democracy, e-democracy has an evident flipside. Social media can dilute and fragment the advocates of a cause, and online tactics can often become undemocratic and uncivil. Questions can include:

- Evaluate the extent to which pressure groups in the UK enhance democracy. (Edexcel-style, 30 marks)
- 'Pressure groups in the UK are fundamentally undemocratic.' Analyse and evaluate this statement. (AQA-style, 25 marks)

The BLM movement provides effective exemplification for pressure group analysis and should be used alongside other relevant factors in assessing contributions to democracy such as equality of influence, resources and the internal democracy of pressure groups themselves.

What next?

Read: the Lammy Review — an insightful appraisal of discrimination and bias in the Criminal Justice System, which can be found at **www.gov.uk/ government/publications/lammy-review-final-report**

Watch: 'Barack Obama takes on 'woke' callout culture: That's not activism', YouTube, 30 October 2019.

Chapter 3

Rights in context: civil liberties campaigns in the 2020s

Focus

All major examination specifications have sections that cover the tensions that exist between individual and collective rights and the extent to which civil liberties are effectively protected in the apparent absence of constitutional safeguards. Within the Edexcel specification there is also a requirement to study the work of at least two contemporary civil liberties movements. There is a range of debates and disagreements over the nature of rights in the UK, including the extent to which campaigning groups contribute to the effective protection of citizens' rights.

Edexcel	UK Politics 1.4	Debates on the extent, limits and tensions within the UK's rights-based culture, including consideration of how individual and collective rights may conflict
AQA	3.1.1.1	Debates about the extent of rights in the UK

This chapter is also useful for Edexcel (1.3) and AQA (3.1.2.4) topics on pressure groups — methods, influence and success.

Context

Competing views of liberty, security and the balance between individual and collective rights are as relevant as ever in the early 2020s. At any time, diverse campaigns to protect, further, challenge and raise awareness of civil liberties are ongoing and Table 3.1 provides a brief snapshot of some of these campaigns in the early 2020s.

With the conflict between individual and collective rights in mind, the debate is increasingly about *who decides*. Are the best arbiters and protectors of civil liberties not elected politicians but unelected judges? In particular, commentators highlight the recent rise in crowdfunded legal action, and the benefits and drawbacks of a potential shift in citizens' ability to access the funds to mount legal challenges over issues they feel strongly about.

Box 3.1   Key definitions

Civil rights: liberties or freedoms granted to citizens within a state. They most often relate to social and political freedoms, such as rights to privacy, voting and legal rights.

Civil liberties differ from **human rights**, as the latter are considered 'inalienable', fundamental to every human being (such as the right to life and freedom from torture) and not within jurisdiction of the state to remove.

Table 3.1 Examples of ongoing civil liberties campaigns in the early 2020s

Campaign area	Explanation
Civil liberties during the health crisis	A wide range of civil liberties groups have highlighted the impact of the coronavirus on rights, particularly through greatly enhanced police powers and the harmful impact on mental health during the lockdowns.
Counter-terrorism	Groups have criticised counter-terror measures, some of which have seen the reintroduction of indefinite detention or the expansion of Terrorism Prevention and Investigation Measures (TPIMs), similar to Control Orders.
Limits to judicial review	Rights groups have expressed concern about government plans to limit the scope of judicial review, which they see as a vital democratic check to ensure effective and lawful governance.
Homelessness	Ensuring awareness of the plight of the homeless, especially during the health crisis, was the objective of several rights groups, especially when some rough sleepers were fined for being outside during the lockdowns despite having nowhere to go.
Immigration and migrants' rights	In the wake of the Windrush scandal that saw long-term UK residents from former Commonwealth countries detained or deported, rights groups continue to campaign for full reform of an immigration system that they say abuses basic human rights.
Mental health and disability	The Coronavirus Act contained provisions allowing local authorities to reduce their social care duties under the Care Act, meaning that disabled people were disproportionately affected (see Case study 1).
Policing	Civil liberties groups continue to campaign against the use of facial recognition software (see Case study 2), discriminatory policing and the misuse of police powers during lockdown.
Soldiers' rights	Civil liberties groups including Liberty continue to campaign for soldiers' rights, especially victims of sexual assault investigated by the military police, as commanding officers are not required to refer allegations to the civilian police.

Case study 1: Campaigns to support disabled people during the lockdown

Campaigning groups such **Disability Rights UK** highlighted the particularly severe impact of lockdown measures on disabled people and others with mental health needs who rely heavily on social care. From March 2020, local authorities were authorised to reduce their provision of social care during the lockdown and up to eight local councils went on to trigger permitted 'easements' of Care Act responsibilities under Schedule 12 of the Coronavirus Act. The councils argued that factors such as staffing complications during the lockdown and complying with health and hygiene guidelines meant that some carer visits and needs assessments had to be postponed.

Disability Rights UK was among several civil rights groups to draw public attention to councils that cut back on their care and services programmes during the lockdown. In highlighting — publicly through media channels and privately through legal channels — the greater stress and potential harm caused to disabled people, Disability Rights UK was successful in ensuring the reversal of all council decisions to ease or halt services prior to the end of June 2020.

In addition, civil liberties groups such as **Turning Point** and **Learning Disability England** challenged the growth of 'do not resuscitate' orders (DNRs) during the lockdown. Many DNRs were unlawfully put in place for disabled people without their families being consulted. Learning Disability England said that almost one-fifth of its members had reported DNRs being placed in their medical records without consultation during March and April 2020. The group campaigned to raise national awareness of the problem, supported families in challenging and reversing unlawful DNRs, and lobbied senior NHS staff and ministers to issue clearer guidelines on the use of DNRs.

Box 3.2 Disability Rights UK

Disability Rights UK is a group representing the needs and interests of disabled people in the UK. The group was formed in 2012 when several disabilities groups merged. It campaigns for independent living, work and education for disabled people and against hate crime, bullying and negative attitudes towards disabled people.

Box 3.3 The greater use of unlawful 'do not resuscitate' orders

National charities have successfully challenged more than a dozen unlawful do not resuscitate orders (DNRs) that were put in place because of the patient's disability rather than due to any serious underlying health risk... In one example, a man in his fifties with sight loss was admitted to hospital after a choking episode and was incorrectly diagnosed with coronavirus. He was discharged the next day with a DNR form giving the reason as his 'blindness and severe learning disabilities'.

Source: 'Coronavirus: unlawful do not resuscitate orders imposed on people with learning disabilities', *The Independent*, June 2020

Case study 2: Challenging facial recognition technology

Among many ongoing campaigns, the civil rights group **Liberty** has long fought against the introduction and proliferation of facial recognition technology. Facial recognition technology compares images captured against a database of images of people on a watch list, including criminal suspects and people of interest. It has been pioneered by forces such as South Wales Police and the Metropolitan Police. Liberty highlighted in November 2019 that a wider roll-out was being based on the completion of just ten trial deployments and in the face of an independent review which concluded that trials had failed to fully consider the impact of the technology on human rights.

Throughout 2019 and 2020, Liberty raised issues such as there being no law regulating the use of facial recognition technology, no public or parliamentary discussion of the impact of the technology on human rights, and that the wider roll-out was occurring in spite of ongoing legal action from civil liberties groups. By mid-2020, Liberty's petition calling for a ban on the use of facial recognition technology in public had been signed by well over 50,000 people.

In September 2019 after a long-running legal dispute, rights campaigner and Cardiff resident Ed Bridges' challenge to South Wales Police's use of facial recognition technology was rejected. But in August 2020, a judgement by the Court of Appeal agreed with Liberty's submissions and found South Wales Police's use of facial recognition technology to be in breach of privacy rights, data protection laws and equality laws. The ground-breaking judgement meant that the police force leading the use of facial recognition on UK streets was required to halt its long-running trial.

Other groups such as **Big Brother Watch** focus their campaigns specifically on challenging what they deem to be excessive surveillance by the state. Tactics related to facial recognition technology include:

- increasing pressure in Parliament to introduce a public bill to ban live facial recognition
- launching local campaigns to encourage councils to oppose facial recognition surveillance
- organising demonstrations to protest against and monitor police activity wherever facial recognition technology is tested or used
- providing legal advice and support to anyone affected by live facial recognition

Box 3.4 Liberty

Liberty is an independent membership organisation that seeks to challenge injustice and defend freedom. It is staffed by campaigners, lawyers and policy experts who 'work together to protect rights and hold the powerful to account'. Liberty provides policy responses to government consultations on a wide range of issues which have implications for human rights and civil liberties. It also submits evidence to parliamentary select committee inquiries and undertakes independent research.

> ### Box 3.5 Facial recognition technology: 'fundamental deficiencies'
>
> In what is the world's first legal challenge to the use of [facial recognition] technology, the judges ruled on Tuesday that there were 'fundamental deficiencies' in the legal framework governing its deployment by South Wales Police, which is the lead police force trialling the technology. The ground-breaking ruling is a major victory for human rights group Liberty and campaigner Ed Bridges who jointly brought the legal action.
>
> Source: 'Police use of facial recognition breaches human rights law, London court rules', *Financial Times*, 11 August 2020

Case study 3: Crowdfunding to widen legal access in the protection of rights

Liberty's 2020 case against South Wales Police was funded through public donations via **CrowdJustice**, a crowdfunding platform that started in the UK in 2015 to improve and widen access to the legal system. The CrowdJustice platform is staffed by UK lawyers who evaluate the various campaigns and challenges brought to them, to establish legal angles and likely success, and then set a financial target for the level of funding required to support necessary legal action.

Recent notable cases funded via CrowdJustice include:

- 2017 — the 'People's Challenge' to the Brexit campaign saw over £170,000 raised from nearly 5,000 donors. The case was finally resolved by the UK Supreme Court and confirmed that an Act of Parliament was needed before Article 50 could be triggered.
- 2018 — the Centre for Women's Justice (CWJ) raised funds via CrowdJustice to support two women who had been sexually assaulted by John Worboys, in opposition to his release. The CWJ campaign led to a reversal of the Parole Board decision and the resignation of the Parole Board chair.
- 2019 — Jolyon Maugham QC, founder of the Good Law Project, crowdfunded over £200,000 from nearly 8,000 donors to mount a legal challenge against Parliament's prorogation — Boris Johnson's 2019 attempt to put Parliament into a recess for up to 5 weeks. The initial challenge was directed to the Advocate General of Scotland and the subsequent finding in Scotland's highest court — that the prorogation was unlawful —was confirmed by the UK Supreme Court soon after.
- 2020 — amid wider media and political pressure, a CrowdJustice campaign was launched immediately after the issuing of the A-level results in August 2020. Many of the grades generated by Ofqual's algorithm were criticised extensively by schools and students for the high number of individual injustices that were caused. Within days, the grades were withdrawn and students received the higher of their centre-assessed (teacher's) grade (CAG) and their Ofqual-awarded grade.

While crowdfunding is well established on the internet, crowdfunding for legal proceedings is relatively new and has risen sharply in recent years on the back of high-profile cases such as the challenges to Brexit. However, even well-funded campaigns can end in failure:

- Private prosecutor Marcus Ball spent a crowdfunded £430,000 in 2019 in a failed bid to have Boris Johnson charged with misconduct in public office for telling 'demonstrable falsehoods during the EU referendum campaign'.
- A recent application for a judicial review of the legality of Article 50 in 2018 attracted over £190,000 but was found in the High Court to be 'hopeless and, for that matter, totally without merit'.

After significant reduction in funding for legal aid since 2012, legal crowdfunding that garners wide support through social network sharing appears to have gone some way towards filling the financial gap. Since its launch in 2015, CrowdJustice alone has seen over £10 million raised for legal proceedings in support of over 1,000 cases.

Concerns remain that legal crowdfunding can encourage spurious, time-consuming or malicious challenges. In particular, there are fears that political matters could be pulled into the legal arena even more frequently. However, others see the legal crowdfunding process as an important development — filling a political participation gap and satisfying a desire among people to act upon something that affects them.

Box 3.6 CrowdJustice and junior doctors' contracts

Chris Day's first Twitter post was fairly standard. 'It feels good to tweet', he wrote. He got two likes. A week later he posted a second time, about a legal challenge to protect junior doctors' whistleblowing rights. Hundreds of people retweeted it. Soon, he marshalled an 'army' of 3,000-odd backers, who chipped in more than £200,000 to his cause. In 2016 the government wrote the right into junior doctors' contracts. It really did feel good to tweet.

Source: 'Crowdfunding is opening up Britain's justice system', *The Economist*, November 2018

Connections and comparisons

- Constitutional arrangements for the protection of civil rights differ greatly between the UK and the USA. Basic civil rights in the USA are constitutionally protected, as the Bill of Rights forms the first ten amendments to the US constitution. In the UK, with neither codified constitution nor entrenched bill of rights, debate remains over the extent to which civil rights are effectively protected. That said, the protection of rights in the USA is far from clear-cut. Federal responsibility for many aspects of political life — such as voting rights — has led to significant differences in rights afforded to US citizens, especially on grounds of race.
- One of the main debates on the protection of civil liberties in the UK concerns the power and status of the body responsible for protecting them: the UK Supreme Court. There is little debate that in the passing of the Human Rights Act (1998) and the creation of the UK Supreme Court (2009) judges have become increasingly prominent in determining the extent of their role in protecting rights against arbitrary rule of government. However, whether this is an advantageous development or not is a topic for debate.

Exam success

Examination questions on this topic may well blend debates on the protection of civil rights in the UK with Britain's wider constitutional arrangements.

- Evaluate the extent to which rights are effectively protected in the UK. (Edexcel-style, 30 marks)
- 'Civil rights are ineffectively protected in the UK.' Analyse and evaluate this statement. (AQA-style, 25 marks)

With the campaigning work of civil liberties groups in mind, students will need to evaluate:

- the implications of the UK's uncodified constitution
- the lack of awareness on the part of UK citizens about their rights
- the power of Parliament to revoke rights depending on circumstances

These factors will need to be balanced by the fact that, in spite of a flexible constitution, many rights are protected by statutes that cover such things as workplace discrimination, and that UK courts are particularly active in asserting and protecting citizens' rights.

What next?

Research: review the latest CrowdJustice cases at **www.crowdjustice.com**

Read: Liberty's campaign against facial recognition technology: **www.libertyhumanrights.org.uk**

Chapter 4

Political parties in the 2020s: funding, fairness and the future

Focus

The roles and functions of political parties feature in all examination specifications. As well as evaluating the development, ideas and impact of the main and smaller parties, and the different party systems in the UK, students need to be able to analyse and evaluate arguments around party funding in light of the most recent evidence. Foremost among debates about the funding of political parties is the extent to which current arrangements are unfair and undemocratic, and whether the advantages of a system of state funding for political parties outweigh the disadvantages.

| Edexcel | UK Politics 2.1 | Political parties — including how the current parties are funded, debates and consequences of the current funding system |
| AQA | 3.1.2.3 | Political parties — including issues and debates around party funding |

Context

During the 2019 general election period, political parties received a total of £30.7 million in registered donations, almost two-thirds of which (63%) were donated to one party: the Conservatives. Consequently, debates and controversies about the fairness of party funding in the UK were thrown into the spotlight again.

Long-established patterns of party funding have seen significant shifts in recent years. Three general elections in the space of 4 years (2015, 2017 and 2019) disrupted the ordinary flow and balance of party funds. Substantial disparities in the capacity of parties to out-spend their opponents, alongside accusations that wealthy donors have become even more influential, have seen arguments for a new way of funding political parties gather pace.

Box 4.1 Key definition

Political parties: organisations formed of like-minded individuals, aiming to secure election victories in constituencies in order to establish a government.

What did the 2019 general election reveal about the state of party funding?

Notable features of party funding in the most recent general election campaign include the fact that the Conservative Party received far more than all the other parties put together during the campaign, and that the number of individuals making donations is declining, though the average donation per individual is rising.

Overall donations to political parties are rising

According to the Electoral Reform Commission, the independent body which oversees elections and regulates political finance in the UK, in 2019 political parties received the largest ever amount in financial donations in 1 year. At over £113 million, 2019's total was more than £40 million higher than in the previous record year — 2017, also a general election year.

Table 4.1 Fourth quarter donations
(1 October–31 December 2019, top five parties)

	Party	Donations accepted (£m)	Public funds received (£)
1	Conservative Party	37.7	67,425
2	Liberal Democrats	13.4	212,627
3	Labour Party	9.8	851,526
4	Brexit Party	7.1	0
5	Green Party	0.4	22,182

Source: www.electoralcommission.org.uk

However, in the 6 weeks before the 2019 general election period, parties received a total of £30.7 million of registered donations. This was 32% less than the £44.9 million received in the 6 weeks before the 2017 general election.

The Conservative Party received the most during the election campaign itself. According to the House of Commons Library paper on political party funding, in 2019 the Conservative Party accumulated just under two-thirds of all donations (£19.4m, 35% less than in 2017), followed by the Labour Party (£5.4m, 47% less) and the Liberal Democrats (£1.3m, 64% less).

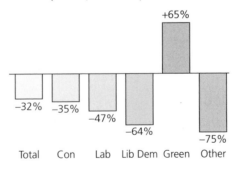

Figure 4.1 Total registered donations by political party — % change from 2017 to 2019

Source: www.commonslibrary.parliament.uk

Notable party funding details in the run-up to the 2019 general election include:

- over £5 million of the Labour Party's £5.4 million in donations was supplied by trade unions
- £13.2 million of the Conservative Party's donations came from individuals
- all of the Brexit Party's £4.2 million in donations was made by individuals
- donations to the Green Parties (registered separately in England and Scotland) increased by 65% from £147,000 in 2017 to £245,000 in 2019.

Box 4.2 **The rise of digital spending**

- In 2015, total spending on leaflets was just over £15 million, while payments to Facebook, Google and Twitter totalled £1.7 million.
- Two years later in 2017, spending on leaflets had declined for the first time in 20 years, to £13.4 million, while payments by the political parties to Facebook, Google, Twitter and Snapchat totalled £4.3 million.
- Estimates by the Electoral Reform Society for the 2019 general election put digital spending by the three main UK-wide parties at almost £10 million. With around £6 million spent on Facebook and just under £3 million on Google, it represents a substantial increase on digital spending compared to the previous general election.

The number of individual donors is falling but the average amount donated is rising

In terms of individual donations, political parties are required to submit quarterly returns to the Electoral Commission. Within these returns, parties report all donations above the £7,500 threshold, and those over £1,500 for local donations.

Overall, the total number of individuals making registered donations to political parties during the general election campaign in 2019 was 266 — 4 times lower than the 1,016 who made individual donations in the 2017 campaign. Yet the average value of each individual donation increased substantially — by almost 3 times from £24,000 in 2017 to over £71,000 in 2019.

Should political parties be funded by the state?

The ever greater amounts donated and the growing gap between parties has intensified the debate about the state funding of political parties. On one side are those who see state funding as a means to eliminate the undemocratic influence of wealthy and corporate donors. On the other side are those who see donating to political parties — for all its imperfections — as a fundamental democratic right.

Five reasons that political parties should be funded by the state

1 There is an urgent need to diminish the influence of 'big money' donations to political parties. From Bernie Ecclestone's £1 million donated to the Labour Party in 1997, to the £8 million donated by Lord Sainsbury to the Liberal Democrats in the last 3 months of the 2019 election campaign, the effect is to undermine trust that the electoral process works in the democratic interests of the many not the few.

Box 4.3 **The Liberal Democrats — breaking fundraising records**

Between 1 October and 31 December 2019, the [Liberal Democrat] party received donations totalling £13,372,664 from 433 donors. That is more than the Labour party received in the same period. A staggering 60% of that total, £8 million, was given to the party by one person, namely Lord (David) Sainsbury, a Labour peer (on leave of absence since 2013) and former supporter of the old SDP. This was the biggest single donation to a political party in UK history. It would be interesting to know what Lord Sainsbury's thoughts are as to his donation vis a vis our performance in the December 2019 general election.

Source: Paul Walter, 'One thing we did really well for the 2019 general election — raising shedloads of dosh', *Liberal Democrat Voice*, 31 March 2020

---

2 It is precisely in times of economic uncertainty, when many are less likely to consider donating to political parties, that fair funding is needed to diminish the influence of wealthy and influential elites. Lord Bamford of JCB donated £3.4 million to the Conservatives in 2019. The company's 'Get Brexit Done' digger received significant publicity during the campaign and Lord Bamford is a legislator in the House of Lords.

3 The influence of the trade unions in support of Labour Party candidates has preserved the hold of the unions over Labour. With 90% of the Labour Party's 2019 campaign funds coming from union support, union influence remains substantial. The Unite trade union alone gave the Labour Party £4.9m in the last quarter of 2019, making its ongoing importance to the Labour Party significant.

Box 4.4 **Unite union reviews financial support for the Labour Party**

The *Daily Express* reported in August 2020 that the Labour Party was 'in crisis' with the Unite union seeking to review donations to the party, allegedly over 'anti-Semitism pay-outs'. Keir Starmer's decision to pay 'six-figure damages' to ex-staffers who claimed the party had not dealt with anti-Semitism angered the Unite leader, Len McCluskey, who said there was 'no doubt' the union's ruling executive would be demanding a review of the millions it donates to the Labour party.

'It's an abuse of members' money,' said Len McCluskey. 'A lot of it is Unite's money, and I'm already being asked all kinds of questions by my executive. It's as though a huge sign has been put up outside the Labour party with "queue here with your writ and get your payment over there".'

Source: adapted from 'Labour in crisis as Unite reviews donations', *Daily Express*, 3 August 2020

---

4 The party funding imbalance is growing. In 2019, the Conservatives surpassed their record of £25 million raised in the lead-up to the 2017 election. In 2019, the fear of a Jeremy Corbyn-led Labour government persuaded many existing

Tory donors to give ever larger sums. Of the top political donors in the UK in 2020, 44 of them financially supported the Conservative Party.

5 The mechanisms are already in place to roll out wider state funding. Expanding Short Money (named after the politician Ted Short who devised the funding formula) to support parliamentary business and research for opposition parties, Cranborne Money, which provides funds to support the main opposition parties in the House of Lords, and policy development grants (which total up to £2 million a year) would all create a fairer and more democratic system of party funding.

Five reasons that political parties should not be funded by the state

1 Citizens should not be barred from donating to causes that they believe in. The fundamental right to support and sustain causes and interests that are important to us is one to be valued and protected. Since political parties have no less a right to the kind of financial support enjoyed by charities, faiths, interest groups or social movements, a system of state-funding for political parties would fly in the face of the most basic principles of a pluralist liberal democracy.

2 Donations are heavily regulated anyway. Legislation including the Electoral Administration Act (2006) and the Political Parties and Elections Act (2009) all responded to growing unease that the decline of broad party memberships allowed wealthy organisations and individuals to wield excessive influence. They introduced a raft of measures to ensure that individual donations are declared and transparent.

3 State funding will serve to entrench existing party strengths. If the criteria for the central funding of parties is based upon historic electoral appeal then established parties will continue to enjoy the lion's share of available funds, potentially colluding to keep out 'new' parties that threaten to dilute their income stream.

4 State-funded parties will be less independent. Ultimately, who owns a political party? Are they to be seen as part of the larger apparatus of the state — like loyal, semi-autonomous agencies? Or as independent entities: alert to the demands of members and voters, able to challenge existing constitutional or governmental arrangements and offer radical solutions where necessary?

5 Who wants their taxes spent on political parties — especially ones they do not support? Should the state really be considering diverting financial resources — many tens of millions of pounds — to political parties? What difference will it make to democracy? To those that suggest money makes a huge difference, and that parties can simply 'out-spend' opponents, in 2019 the Liberal Democrats spent half as much again as the Labour Party, yet their seats reduced from 12 to 11.

Connections and comparisons

- There are some clear democratic principles involved in this topic — that of our basic rights to support causes that we believe in, whether financially or otherwise. In terms of the key principles of democracy, participation, engagement and representation, it is likely that any system of state funding would disconnect parties even from their natural supporters, increasing levels of apathy and mistrust among voters and eroding the vital requirement for parties to offer attractive, relevant and appealing policies and proposals to their supporters.
- The issue of campaign finance in the USA is an explosive one. With so many elections taking place at local, state and federal level — electing representatives to school boards, city halls, state legislatures, judicial benches and more — accurately calculating the amount raised and spent is an impossibly complex task. For example, the total cost of the 2020 presidential and congressional elections is estimated to be in excess of $14 billion, more than double the $6.5 billion spending during the previous presidential/congressional election cycle in 2016.

Exam success

Exam questions on this topic are likely to require students to balance the advantages and disadvantages of state funding alongside the impact and consequences of the significant sums spent in the UK — although clearly sums that are far less substantial than those spent in the USA. Questions may be framed as follows:

- Evaluate the extent to which political parties in the UK should be funded by the state. (Edexcel-style, 30 marks)
- 'Political parties in the UK should be funded by the state.' Analyse and evaluate this statement. (AQA-style, 25 marks)

The best responses will include:

- the functions played by parties and the way that state funding could enhance those functions
- the decline of mass membership and the growing influence of wealthy donors
- the consequences of the links between Labour and the unions, and the Conservatives and 'corporate' donors
- the complications of how to calculate state funding and on what basis
- the disconnect that could occur between citizens and parties, if parties were funded by the state

What next?

Read: the House of Commons Library report 'General Election 2019: Which party received the most donations?', January 2020, which can be found on **https://commonslibrary.parliament.uk**

Read: the Electoral Commission's report 'Record year and quarter for political party donations and loans in Great Britain', February 2020, on **www.electoralcommission.org.uk**

Chapter 5

The influence of the media: is the BBC biased, and does it matter?

Focus

Understanding the relevance of media influence through bias and persuasion is an important area of all examination specifications. Students will need a thorough knowledge of the ways in which both traditional media (newspapers, radio and television) and 'new' media (social media platforms and online news channels) shape issues and events and influence social and political developments.

Edexcel	UK Politics 4.2	The influence of the media
AQA	3.1.2.2– 3.1.2.4	The influence of the media on politics (elections, pressure groups and political parties)

Context

As one of the biggest global media brands with an active worldwide audience of over 500 million, more than 26 million domestic TV licence payers and over 40 million daily users in the UK, even in spite of ever greater media diversity, the BBC remains one of the biggest single influencers of political views and opinions. Consequently, its output, coverage and questions of bias and persuasion are especially relevant to students of politics.

With several interlinked issues and controversies coming to the fore in the early 2020s, the influence of the BBC has come under greater scrutiny than ever before. Among other things, the BBC was accused of being out-of-touch with its core 'middle England' audience, too narrow in the range of social and political opinions of its staff, and too keen to follow social and political fashions. That said, the corporation has long faced accusations that its coverage of many contested areas of politics, religion, ethics, and foreign affairs is biased.

- Many on the right of the political spectrum see the BBC as emphatically left-wing. Such claims stem from a belief that it is controlled by left-leaning liberals and that residual anti-Thatcher sentiment from the 1980s has turned into entrenched anti-Conservative bias. BBC presenter and historian Andrew Marr recently asserted that 'the BBC is not impartial or neutral. It has a liberal bias'.
- On the contrary, those on the left find proof of the BBC's right-leaning pro-establishment bias in its seemingly staunch support for the union of the United Kingdom and its preoccupation with the monarchy. Left-wing columnist and *Guardian* writer Owen Jones recently declared that 'the BBC is stacked full of right-wingers'.

Box 5.1 **Key definition**

Media bias: selection and coverage of events and stories that may contravene expected standards of journalism. Government influence, censorship, market forces, audience preferences and the subjective approaches of staff are all potential drivers of media bias.

Why is the influence of the BBC significant?

The BBC has played a prominent role in British cultural life for a century. Established by Royal Charter in 1920, it is the world's oldest broadcaster with a current staff totalling over 35,000. The corporation is funded primarily by the television licence fee, which is charged to all British households and organisations that use any type of televisual equipment to watch its broadcasts. The BBC's annual revenue, including proceeds from international broadcasting, is around £5 billion a year.

Box 5.2 **The reach of the BBC**

Let's start with the facts. Right now, the BBC is the most-used media organisation in the UK, by around 40 million people every day. We reach the most people — more than 9 out of 10 adults every week, and more than 8 out of 10 children.

Source: 'Why the BBC matters', Lord Hall, former director-general of the BBC, www.politicshome.com

The BBC has sought to remain both relevant and valuable in the way that it operates, with new initiatives such as the Local Democracy Reporting Service seeking to inform and connect the public, highlighting issues that affect them.

Box 5.3 **The Local Democracy Reporting Service**

Launched 2 years ago, the Local Democracy Reporting Service works in partnership with regional newspapers and local media to hold local politicians and public institutions to account. Within 2 years the Local Democracy Reporting Service had produced more than 100,000 public interest stories, raising a whole range of issues that may not otherwise have been heard.

The corporation's influence cannot be understated. In the words of the outgoing BBC director-general Lord Hall in August 2020, it sits 'at the fulcrum of big societal changes at a time in which people are questioning and challenging every aspect of their own lives and more widely too'.

That said, the BBC's coverage and approach has been the subject of dispute for as long as the corporation has existed. In the 1980s it was particularly criticised by right-leaning opponents for its 'unpatriotic' coverage of the Falklands War and branded the 'Bolshevik Broadcasting Company' by Conservative opponents, with Margaret Thatcher declaring that she had 'fought three general elections against the BBC'.

More recent years have seen sustained criticism, with the BBC most often accused of breaching its own guidelines over content, bias and impartiality. In the early 2020s, prompted by its 100-year anniversary as much as by a quick succession of controversies — which also included the salaries paid to its leading earners, equal pay disputes and TV licence fee rows — the BBC's role, relevance, leadership and funding came under the spotlight.

With the influence, reach and responsibilities of the BBC in mind, an examination of the controversies that may have a significant bearing on its credibility, reliability and integrity are well worthwhile.

Is the BBC impartial?

The BBC's charter requires its output, particularly its journalism, to be impartial. While impartiality does not have to mean 'neutrality', several senior journalists including *Newsnight* presenters have made comments on political matters that have received criticism.

Box 5.4 **Editorial guidelines, section 4: Impartiality**

The BBC is committed to achieving due impartiality in all its output. This commitment is fundamental to our reputation, our values and the trust of audiences...

We must be inclusive, considering the broad perspective and ensuring that the existence of a range of views is appropriately reflected. It does not require absolute neutrality on every issue or detachment from fundamental democratic principles, such as the right to vote, freedom of expression and the rule of law.

Source: **www.bbc.co.uk/editorialguidelines/guidelines/impartiality**

Case study 1: The BBC and the Dominic Cummings saga, May 2020

It is often highlighted that the overwhelming proportion of breaches of impartiality in recent years have been anti-Conservative or left-leaning in nature.

Such criticism seemed particularly relevant when Emily Maitlis was replaced as the host of an episode of *Newsnight* in May 2020 immediately after her attack on the government's handling of Dominic Cummings' lockdown trip to Durham.

In late May 2020, Emily Maitlis turned her BBC *Newsnight* introduction into an extended monologue, appearing to offer a personal view on the situation:

> Dominic Cummings broke the rules — the country can see that, and it's shocked the government cannot. The longer ministers and the prime minister insist he worked within them, the more angry the response to the scandal is likely to be... He made those who struggled to keep to the rules feel like fools and has allowed many more to assume they can flout them... The prime minister knows all this and has chosen to ignore it.

The 'Maitlis monologue' went viral on social media, with support for the *Newsnight* presenter focused on the defence that one of the central roles of effective news journalism — whether via the BBC or not — is to provide effective scrutiny and to hold political leaders (in this case the government and paid advisors) to account. Nevertheless, the introduction provoked a substantial backlash. In response to more than 40,000 complaints in just 2 days, the BBC issued a statement soon after:

> We've reviewed the entirety of last night's *Newsnight*, including the opening section, and while we believe the programme contained fair, reasonable and rigorous journalism, we feel that we should have done more to make clear the introduction was a summary of the questions we would examine, with all the accompanying evidence, in the rest of the programme. As it was, we believe the introduction we broadcast did not meet our standards of due impartiality. Our staff have been reminded of the guidelines.

However, at the other end of the spectrum Laura Kuenssberg, political editor of BBC News, faced equally fierce criticism and reproach when she appeared to defend Dominic Cummings on Twitter. Kuenssberg shared a rebuttal within minutes of the story breaking, tweeting: 'Source says his trip was within guidelines'. Her further explanatory tweets were met with sustained hostility — 'absolute nonsense' replied Piers Morgan, and 'lies, propaganda and spin' tweeted philosopher A. C. Grayling.

Perceptions of the public

The question of impartiality remains a contentious one. The BBC's own guidelines commit it to 'applying due impartiality to all subjects' yet also to exercise 'editorial freedom to produce content about any subject, at any point on the spectrum of debate, as long as there are good editorial reasons for doing so'.

Its coverage of contested issues places the BBC in the firing line from all sides, evidenced in a 2018 opinion poll by BMG Research which found that 40% of the British public think that the BBC is politically partisan, though accusations of bias are evenly split between those who believe it leans to the left or right. More recent research commissioned by Ofcom revealed that just 59% of those surveyed agreed that the BBC News was impartial, comparing unfavourably with levels received by ITV News (61%) and Sky News (64%).

Consequently, the question of the impartiality of the BBC — as the UK's state-owned broadcaster — remains a live one for students of politics.

Has social media use undermined the integrity of the BBC?

In the summer of 2020, head of editorial standards David Jordan criticised some BBC presenters' use of social media when questioned by the House of Lords communication and digital committee. David Jordan said that social media use enables presenters to reach audiences that do not otherwise engage with the corporation, particularly the young. However, he also acknowledged that social media can become 'addictive for some of our journalists' and that guidance on the use of social media is sometimes breached.

Some newsreaders and presenters are prolific users of Twitter and have come under greater scrutiny with critics of their online activity arguing that it conflicts with the required impartiality of their role as presenters. However, accusations of the improper use of social media often appear politically motivated and tenuous at best.

For example, Huw Edwards, the BBC newsreader, was criticised for 'liking' a pro-Labour video shared by a Labour activist and originally posted by trade union GMB in December 2019. The clip included the slogan 'Vote Labour for the National Health Service' near the end. Edwards apologised, saying that he did not watch the video 'to the end', but said he would not apologise for 'supporting the NHS'.

That said, the new BBC director-general Tim Davie explained to the Commons Culture Select Committee in September 2020 that 'we will be able to take people off Twitter' if they did not comply with soon-to-be-drawn-up social media guidelines on impartiality. Gary Lineker — who has long irritated opponents with his anti-Conservative anti-Brexit posts — responded with a 'crying with laughter' emoji, tweeting 'I think only Twitter can take people off Twitter'.

Is the BBC too metropolitan and 'woke'?

The BBC has received sustained criticism for its perceived desire to follow social and political fashions too aggressively, and at the expense of its 'more traditional' audience. The term 'woke' and the accusations that stem from it appear to have stuck somewhat, especially over what is believed by some to be the corporation's sustained hostility towards Brexit, its perceived anti-Trump bias, its strong advocacy of certain theories on climate change, and its believed reluctance to upset the liberal mainstream.

| Box 5.7 | **The weaponisation of woke** |

[According to] the Merriam-Webster dictionary definition, woke means 'aware of and actively attentive to important facts and issues (especially issues of racial and social justice)', but today we are more likely to see it being used as a stick with which to beat people who aspire to such values, often wielded by those who don't recognise how un-woke they are, or are proud of the fact.

Source: Steve Rose, 'How the word "woke" was weaponised by the right',
The Guardian, January 2020

The BBC's perceived desire to be seen as 'on trend' has led it to make what some might consider questionable decisions. Yet many such decisions — ones that have received sustained coverage from news outlets often in direct competition with the BBC — are considerably less clear-cut than they might appear on first examination.

Case study 2: Singing at the Proms

For some, the decision to cancel the singing of the words of 'Land of Hope and Glory' and 'Rule Britannia!' at the Last Night of the Proms was symptomatic of the corporation's betrayal of unfashionable, patriotic middle England. It was a decision hidden under the cover of 'health measures' yet indicative of the corporation's desperation — in relation to songs associated with colonialism, imperialism and slavery — not to offend the liberal left audience it courts.

Boris Johnson opposed the BBC's decision to play instrumental versions of 'Land of Hope and Glory' and 'Rule, Britannia!', saying 'I think it's time we stopped our cringing embarrassment about our history.'

However, many others — including anti-racism campaigners, academics and political commentators — maintained that the controversy was an entirely artificial one, and merely more of the same condemnation and deliberate misrepresentation of the BBC as liberally biased by the Conservative Party and right-wing newspapers.

Recently, Naga Munchetty, the BBC Breakfast presenter, was found to have breached guidelines over her comments about a 'go home' tweet sent by President Trump to four US congresswomen of colour. 'Every time I have been told, as a woman of colour,' said Naga Munchetty on BBC Breakfast in July 2019, 'to go back to where I came from, that was embedded in racism'. She added that she was 'absolutely furious' at Trump's choice of words in his tweet. However, the BBC's decision that Munchetty's comments had breached guidelines was later reversed by director-general Lord Hall who maintained that he did not 'think Naga's words were sufficient to merit a partial uphold of the complaint around the comments she made'.

Other arguments against the BBC include its London-bias. Lord Hall himself admitted that he thought the corporation could do better and 'do a big push to get more out of London', estimating that in terms of staff and spending 'we are

50% in London and 50% out of London. I think we can do much better than that. I think we can get to 70% out of London, and that changes the dynamic of the discussions you can have'.

Connections and comparisons

- *The Guardian* reported in August 2020 that 'efforts are under way' to launch a Fox News-style opinionated current affairs television station in Britain. For many, the possibility that news media in the USA — where political division is even more pronounced between conservative Republicans and liberal Democrats — could be aped in the UK would be an unwelcome step.
- In the USA, there is evidence to suggest that polarisation in the use and trust of media sources has widened in the past 5 years. In an era of increasingly opinionated current affairs, Republicans have become progressively more alienated from most established news sources, while confidence in them among Democrats remains stable.
- Adfontes Media (**www.adfontesmedia.com**) analyses and rates the news in the USA for bias and reliability using rigorous methodology and a 'politically balanced team of analysts'. *Ad Fontes* is Latin for 'to the source'. The organisation looks directly at every item of news output and provides information and resources to allow judgements to be made on the reliability and bias of each piece of news encountered.

Exam success

Questions on media influence involving evidence of BBC impartiality, persuasion and bias are likely to link with wider questions on the extent to which media influence undermines or enhances democracy in the UK. Questions might include:

- Evaluate the extent to which media influence in the UK undermines democracy. (Edexcel-style, 30 marks)
- 'Media influence in the UK undermines democracy.' Analyse and evaluate this statement. (AQA-style, 25 marks)

In addition to an evaluation of the BBC's role, students will also need to develop the extent to which 'new' forms of media, especially consumed via social media platforms, can influence and persuade.

What next?

Read: 'The BBC is under scrutiny. Here's what research tells about its role in the UK', Professor Rasmus Kleis Nielsen, Dr Anne Schulz and Dr Richard Fletcher, 28 February 2020, **https://reutersinstitute.politics.ox.ac.uk**

Research: Ofcom's 2020 report, 'News consumption in the UK', 13 August 2020 on **www.ofcom.org.uk**

Chapter 6

Devolution: the state of the union — stronger than ever, or a dangerous mess?

Focus

Devolution features within all examination specifications. Students require knowledge of the differing roles, powers and impact of the devolved institutions in Scotland, Wales, Northern Ireland and England, and analysis of whether the decentralisation of power over the last 20 years should be 'taken further'. Students will need to evaluate whether unresolved issues relating to the asymmetric devolution of power within the UK, and the level of autonomy of the English regions — and indeed of England itself — could be constitutionally settled in a way that results in a fully federal United Kingdom or national independence.

Edexcel	UK Government 1.3	The role and powers of the devolved bodies in the UK, and the impact of devolution on the UK
AQA	3.1.1.5	Devolution: the roles, powers and responsibilities of the different devolved bodies in the UK; impact of devolution on government of the UK

Context

On 23 June 2020, marking his first full year in Number 10, the UK prime minister visited Scotland. Boris Johnson's visit, along with his post-crisis financial pledge to Scotland as part of a plan to help Britain 'bounce back stronger together', received mixed reviews north of the border. Scottish first minister Nicola Sturgeon accused the prime minister of 'celebrating a pandemic that has taken thousands of lives' and maintained that the borrowing powers of an independent Scotland would have been just as effective. Additionally, and in the context of ongoing debate about the process of devolution:

- In the wake of the health crisis, extra money was promised to all national regions, with total budget rises of at least £6.5 billion for Scotland, £4 billion for Wales and £2.2 billion for Northern Ireland. However, concerns over the UK's disjointed response to the pandemic, particularly as regions imposed and eased their lockdowns at different rates, remained.
- Boris Johnson was put under pressure about the potential for a substantial Scottish National Party (SNP) landslide in the 2021 Scottish parliamentary elections to reflect the steady growth in support for Scottish independence. The prime minister reiterated the view that the 2014 referendum was meant to settle the matter for a generation and asserted that the union remained 'stronger than ever'.

- The prime minister's visit to Scotland focused upon economic rather than health policies since responsibilities for health are devolved to the regions. In its immediate response to the coronavirus health threat, the UK government had found itself in charge of England alone, prompting a revival of the question over England's constitutional future.

Box 6.1 Key definitions

Asymmetric devolution: uneven transfer of powers and responsibilities to the regions, which has taken place at different times and to different degrees in the last 20 years. While this has emphasised the constitutional flexibility of the UK, it has also had a destabilising effect and been the cause of governing confusion and conflict.

A **fully federal United Kingdom** would see the relationship between central and regional governments formally settled. Instead of the UK parliament retaining ultimate sovereignty, powers would be constitutionally shared and entrenched. Similar to the USA, economic, foreign and defence policies could be retained by a UK government, while most aspects of domestic and social policies would be controlled in the regions.

To what extent was the UK's devolved response to the health crisis disjointed?

Right across the globe, citizens were required to adapt to changing regulations as measures were introduced to tackle the pandemic. But unlike in most other states, the health crisis exposed the UK's awkward internal relationships and often conflicted responsibilities for vital aspects of citizens' lives — especially those of health, security, education, public transport and in the relationships between central, regional, and local administrations.

Table 6.1 Devolved and non-devolved responsibilities in the UK

Major powers of the devolved bodies	Major powers reserved to Westminster
Health and social policy	Defence, national security and foreign policy
Education — schools and universities	Economic policy and monetary systems
Justice, policing and prisons	Employment law
Aspects of taxation (e.g. variations to income tax)	Social security (with some welfare responsibilities devolved to the regions)
Culture (e.g. sport and tourism)	Immigration policy and relations with the EU

Advocates of devolution point to regional government that is more responsive, to representatives that are more accountable, to voters who are more engaged and to localised legislative initiatives that have enhanced citizens' lives. Detractors highlight the strain and uncertainty within the UK's governing arrangements, and the fact that even during a health crisis, ongoing clashes and disagreements reflect the lack of constitutional clarity at the heart of the modern UK state. Notable regional inconsistencies over the course of 2020 included:

- In May, England moved to the slogan 'Stay alert' while Scotland, Wales and Northern Ireland continued with 'Stay home'. Before the UK government's announcement, the Scottish first minister had criticised the policy change and emphasised that a relaxation too soon could prove to be 'catastrophic'.
- The Scottish first minister and UK prime minister clashed over the possibility of quarantine arrangements for people crossing the border between England and Scotland as the lockdown eased in June.
- English day-trippers — potentially unaware of lockdown policy divergences — were challenged and turned away from Wales by local police.
- In Northern Ireland there was sustained disagreement over policy emanating from London especially among nationalists within the regional assembly. With an infection rate substantially lower than the rest of the UK, Northern Ireland followed a different path out of lockdown to that of other UK regions.
- There was significant criticism of policy differences between England and Wales, particularly the imposition of a 'firebreak' lockdown that covered the whole of Wales in October 2020, at a time when the rest of the UK had not imposed one.
- In London, it was unclear as to whether the enforcement of health, hygiene and social distancing measures on public transport was the responsibility of UK ministers or the capital's mayor.
- Residents of Manchester confronted the prospect of a lengthier lockdown at the suggestion of the city's mayor. Yet despite significantly different rates of virus transmission in the northwest, there was little regional autonomy to impose (June 2020) or resist (October 2020) stricter measures.
- In August 2020, Scotland and Wales were said to have 'overruled London' in their demands that quarantine measures for some travellers to the UK be introduced 24 hours earlier. There was further confusion in September when Wales and Scotland introduced quarantine measures for those arriving from Portugal, but England and Northern Ireland held back from restrictions.

For many commentators, the UK's disjointed response was caused as much by decision-making that was too *centralised* (and too distant) to be responsive to local and regional variations in the impact of the virus, as it was by government that was too *decentralised* to develop a co-ordinated response to the lack of protective equipment, the setting up of national testing regimes or of workable contact tracing systems.

Box 6.2	**Coronavirus emergency has exposed devolution as a dangerous mess**

Of Covid-19's many legacies, among the least discussed but most important is the realisation that the British state is dysfunctional and our constitution a mess. The way we are governed is mired in confusion caused by a lack of clarity about where power really lies.

Source: Nick Timothy, joint Downing Street chief of staff to prime minister Theresa May, *Daily Telegraph*, 17 May 2020

Centralised government may have served effectively and decisively in times of national emergency, not least during the Second World War, but the UK state that faced the global health pandemic in 2020 was unrecognisable compared to that of the 1930s: far more complex, fragmented and diverse. The devolved administrations, local authorities and semi-autonomous healthcare trusts that now make up the modern UK state mean that rapid and co-ordinated action, of the type that requires high levels of inter-governmental trust and co-operation, is extremely difficult.

Needless to say, decentralised government worked better upon its introduction in the late 1990s, at a time when the Labour Party ruled in London, Edinburgh and Cardiff and a phone call could 'fix' most problems. Relations between regions in the 2020s are more divided and antagonistic. Added to this, while crisis powers need to sit centrally in order to maximise an emergency response, the pandemic was health-related, and the response was therefore devolved.

However:
- The Coronavirus Act drawn up in March 2020 required deep cross-nation collaboration, reflecting a process and an outcome that was commended by the Institute for Government as that of a 'much more mature federal system'.
- New cross-nation committees dedicated to the pandemic required devolved ministers to meet increasingly effectively, and several times a day. Beneath the superficial disagreements, the differences in national strategies were found to be relatively small.
- The Chief Medical Officers from each devolved nation sat on the Scientific Advisory Group for Emergencies (SAGE) which guided national policies.
- Much of the effective pre- and post-pandemic infrastructure — such as the British Army running mobile testing units and the Joint Biosecurity Centre operating as an outbreak monitoring unit — covered the whole of the UK.

Has the health crisis made Scottish independence more likely?

Epidemics throughout history have often led people to turn inward, seeking to protect and defend their immediate interests. This appeared to have been a feature of the 'border clash' of June 2020. When the Scottish first minister refused to rule out the option of quarantine for English visitors to Scotland, the prime minister criticised the possibility as 'absolutely astonishing and shameful'.

The steady rise in support for Scottish independence predates the health crisis but it would be remarkable if the pandemic did not have an impact upon it. However, some might argue that rather than advancing the cause of independence, the social, economic and political upheaval of the health crisis may be so prolonged that the appetite for the intense disruption of separation will be severely diminished.

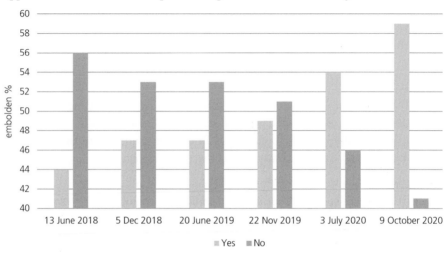

Figure 6.1 Polling data responses to the question: should Scotland be an independent country?

Source: adapted from **www.whatscotlandthinks.org**

Table 6.2 Has the health crisis made Scottish independence more likely?

YES	NO
The immediate post-crisis consensus was that Scottish first minister Nicola Sturgeon had handled it 'better' than prime minister Boris Johnson. Opinion polls in Scotland consistently indicated that Sturgeon had proved herself to be a highly effective and reassuring communicator during the pandemic.	With the responsibility for public health north of the border lying with the Scottish government, there is little evidence that the worst effects of the pandemic were managed any more effectively in Scotland. Scottish care homes experienced a far higher mortality rate than those in England and the rest of the UK, and health policies were broadly similar.
Boris Johnson had declared himself 'minister of the union' yet the lockdown delayed his first visit north of the border since 2019's general election until late June 2020. Despite the prime minister's apparent 'toxicity' to many Scottish voters, the perceived risks to the union were considered too great to continue stalling on a formal visit.	'We are here for each other in sickness and in health' declared Boris Johnson in June 2020. Irrespective of public feelings for Westminster-based administrations, the post-crisis viability of an independent Scotland has been dealt a major blow, especially if future prosperity was to have been based on oil, the price of which has been highly unstable.

YES	NO
The economic recovery is widely considered likely to be more contentious and protracted than the measures put in place to tackle the health crisis itself. However, supporters of independence refute the claim that Scotland could not have handled the crisis without the UK, reassured by the number of small European countries that coped with the coronavirus effectively.	The economic strength of a united UK has been the basis for most unionist arguments — the UK's highly integrated economy; the fact that Scotland would have to establish a new currency and would be smaller and more susceptible to economic shocks. The crisis served to increase co-dependence with over 900,000 Scottish workers furloughed and reliant on UK-backed schemes.
If the 2021 Scottish parliamentary elections return the SNP — campaigning on the platform of a second independence referendum, following effective government during the health crisis — with an even greater majority, it would be very difficult for Westminster to continue to deny the Scottish people the referendum that they had voted for.	Beneath the antagonistic spin, the health crisis is seen by many to have pulled the union closer together. The response to the emergency required levels of inter-governmental cross-border co-operation that had not been seen before. For some, the health crisis revealed just how inextricably linked the UK really is.

Box 6.4 Is the union stronger than ever?

In Scotland, the UK Treasury has protected over 900,000 jobs and granted thousands of businesses loans; the UK's armed forces have airlifted critically ill patients from some of the most remote communities, helped convert the temporary hospitals and ran mobile testing sites; and the Department of Health and Social Care has procured millions of pieces of PPE to keep Scottish frontline workers safe. This is on top of £4.6 billion we have given straight to the Scottish administration to help tackle coronavirus.

Source: www.gov.uk, 23 July 2020

What next for the government of a post-pandemic England?

With the wider infrastructure of state frozen in lockdown, the devolved matters of health and education came to the fore, revealing the UK government to be in charge of England alone — a governing region for which there is neither constitutional foundation nor widespread public support. While the current government of England is based on a Conservative-backed majority of English seats, an uneasy truce exists. But in the event of an alternative — for example, a Westminster government made up of a Labour and SNP coalition facing a Conservative opposition that is supported by a majority of English seats — a crisis of legitimacy could ensue.

Box 6.5 **The state we're in: how the pandemic has exposed the institutional failings of British governance.**

The multi-layered and unbalanced system of devolution that has grown, in fits and starts, over the past two decades across the UK leaves the governance of England opaque and incoherent. And this has been laid bare as the crisis has deepened.

Source: Michael Kenny, Professor of Public Policy, University of Cambridge, *New Statesman*, June 2020

During the pandemic, central government politicians and advisors were immersed in complex UK-wide matters, overlooking the specific national interests of England. Notwithstanding its metro mayors, London assembly, police and crime commissioners, various combined authorities, and devolved legislation such as the 2016 Cities and Local Government Devolution Act, it seemed clear to many that England lacked appropriate regional authorities to wield proper governing responsibilities in the face of a crisis.

There is little doubt that a void remains around English government, one that did not need a pandemic to reveal but that nevertheless became all too obvious as the crisis unfolded. Before the health crisis, the Queen's Speech of December 2019 provided detail of a future White Paper that would set out the government's commitment to 'full devolution across England so that every part of our country has the power to shape its own destiny' but in September 2020, the *Financial Times* reported that the plans had been 'shelved'.

Box 6.6 **'Levelling-up' agenda in question as shake-up of local government also scaled back**

Plans for the biggest shake-up in English local government for more than 30 years have been delayed, raising fresh questions over the government's commitment to 'level up' prosperity across England. The White Paper on devolution and local recovery, which was expected this month, has been shelved until next year as the government prioritises battling Covid-19, according to people with knowledge of the situation.

Source: 'Plans for further English devolution shelved until next year', *Financial Times*, 30 September 2020

For most constitutional commentators, while a competent central authority will always be required — seen most clearly during the crisis in the speed and effectiveness with which the wages of millions of 'furloughed' workers were underwritten — from England's point of view, the current crisis has revealed that the unitary state has 'run its course' and should be replaced by more effective and responsive levels of regional government across England.

Comparisons and connections

- The global nature of the pandemic provides some fascinating and applicable comparisons. Many commentators cited Germany's successful response to the health pandemic. Germany's medical system is highly decentralised, but its crisis response was guided by a national pandemic plan.
- On the other hand, the American response was characterised by an initial dismissal of the seriousness of the health crisis followed by extensive miscommunication between federal and state levels. Most state governors utilised their constitutional powers to determine policy within their own states, largely in isolation from one another and from national efforts. Governors Andrew Cuomo (New York), Mike DeWine (Ohio) and Gavin Newsom (California) all drew praise for their swift action in the face of the crisis. State governors who followed Trump's early inaction, such as Ron DeSantis (Florida), received severe criticism for their slowness to lock down their states.

Exam success

The devolution topic should be tackled in its own right, but also as part of the ongoing process of constitutional reform, particularly in terms of the decentralisation of decision-making power in the UK and with reference to recent developments and challenges. Questions on devolution may be framed as follows:

- Evaluate the extent to which devolution in the UK has failed. (Edexcel-style, 30 marks)
- 'The advantages of devolution in the UK outweigh the disadvantages.' Analyse and evaluate this statement. (AQA-style, 25 marks)

The best responses will provide analysis and evaluation which includes specific information on the role, power and impact of the devolved bodies in Scotland, Wales and Northern Ireland. Analysis will balance the strengths of greater accountability and government responsiveness with the drawbacks of inefficiency, expense and disjointed policies. Top answers may include issues related to England being 'left behind' and demonstrate a thorough understanding of the differences between devolution and federalism.

What next?

Read: House of Commons Briefing Paper (Number 07029, 26 March 2020), 'Devolution to local government in England' by Mark Sandford

Read: Institute for Government's 'English devolution: How governments can successfully decentralise control'. Go to **www.instituteforgovernment.org. uk/our-work/devolution** and click on 'English devolution'.

Visit: University College London's Constitution Unit: Devolution in England, **www.ucl.ac.uk/constitution-unit/research/research-archive/nations-regions-archive/devolution-england**

Chapter 7

Parliament: the House of Lords — too big, too partisan and time for change?

Focus

The composition, selection, functions and powers of the House of Lords feature in all examination specifications. Students are required to evaluate the different types of peers and the selection process to appoint them, and to compare the functions and powers of the Commons and the Lords. For instance, while the primary role of members of the House of Commons (MPs) is to represent constituents in the process of holding the government to account — debating, voting and legislating accordingly — the Lords play a prominent role in revising (and delaying) legislation which means that their party-political composition is significant.

Edexcel	UK Government 2.1–2.4	Including: the House of Lords — structure, role, selection of members; the extent to which its main functions are fulfilled; debates about relative powers of the two houses
AQA	3.1.1.2	Including: the House of Lords — role, influence and significance of peers

Context

On 31 July 2020 Boris Johnson's long-awaited dissolution list of new appointments to the House of Lords was made public. Dissolution lists are often more controversial than peerages announced at other times as their timing, drawn up just ahead of a general election — though often only made public several months later — means they provide an opportunity for prime ministers to reward party donors, close friends or outgoing colleagues or to repay political favours.

The Life Peerages Act 1958 allowed for the appointment of 'life' peers in a bid to invigorate and modernise the second chamber. Later in the twentieth century, the Labour Party delivered on its 1997 election manifesto promise to end 'the right of hereditary peers to sit and vote in the House of Lords'. The House of Lords Act 1999 reduced the chamber's size from 1,330 in 1999 to fewer than 700 the following year. Since then, further reforms to abolish, elect or fully appoint a second chamber have consistently stalled, and appointments remain almost entirely in the hands of the prime minister.

For controversy, Boris Johnson's dissolution list did not disappoint. Critics pointed to the number: 36 new appointments further swelled the Lords at greater cost. For others the objection was the largely unregulated process of appointment itself. For others still, targets were the new peers themselves: according to the *New Statesman* it was a list made up of 'cronies, controversialists, and cricketers' who joined a second chamber now 'more than eight times the size of the US Senate'.

Even staunch critics of the Lords recognise that much good work is done there. Yet recent appointments have brought the role, purpose and future of an unelected, unrepresentative and unaccountable second chamber into the political spotlight again.

Box 7.1 Key definitions

House of Lords: the unelected chamber within the UK's bicameral legislature. It consists largely of life peers, most of them 'ennobled' for their expertise in a wide range of fields. The power of the Lords is largely limited to the revision or delay of legislation passed through the Commons.

House of Lords Act 1999: widely seen as the largest single piece of legislation to affect Parliament's composition. It removed over 600 hereditary peers — those who inherited their seats — leaving just 92 hereditary peers under an 'interim' arrangement and 550 life peers.

Dissolution list: the dissolution of Parliament in the weeks preceding a general election is accompanied by a list of nominees to receive honours from the monarch.

Why was Boris Johnson's dissolution list controversial?

Described by some critics as 'outrageous', Boris Johnson's dissolution list appeared to flout the developing cross-party consensus that the House of Lords should be reduced in size. The list of 36 new peers included millionaire Conservative party donor Michael Spencer, personal advisors to the prime minister such as Eddie Lister and ex-colleagues of the prime minister such as journalists Veronica Wadley and Charles Moore. Some appointments that drew particular attention included:

- Boris Johnson's personal friend Evgeny Lebedev, owner of the *Evening Standard* and son of Alexander Lebedev, a Russian businessman and former KGB agent.
- Prompting accusations of 'the worst kind of cronyism' (cronyism refers to the appointment of friends and associates to positions of office), his brother and former MP Jo Johnson was appointed.
- Claire Fox, a former Brexit Party MEP, who has proved to be a highly controversial figure in the causes she has supported.

Box 7.2 The selection of peers

From 2000, appointments to the House of Lords have been vetted by the independent House of Lords Appointments Commission (HOLAC). Most recommendations to HOLAC are made by the main political parties, able to 'top up' the Lords to ensure broad party-political balance. Prime ministers approve all nominees.

Critics further pointed out that Boris Johnson had used the opportunity to defy long-standing traditions of appointment and snub worthy recipients who would have made valuable contributions. Examples that reflect the prime minister's idiosyncratic list include:

- In defiance of centuries of parliamentary tradition, the outgoing speaker of the House of Commons John Bercow — a thorn in the sides of Brexit-supporting parliamentarians for several years — was not nominated for a peerage.
- Former governor of the Bank of England Mark Carney, outgoing MP and deputy leader of the Labour Party Tom Watson, and of course former Labour leader Jeremy Corbyn were not nominated, yet all were touted by some as likely to have made telling contributions within a second chamber.

However, at a time of considerable social and political change, many have defended the number and the composition of the prime minister's list. Several appointments were Labour peers, crossbenchers or non-affiliated, though the vast majority were Conservatives — many of them Brexit-supporting allies of the prime minister. The appointments are viewed by some as necessary to mirror the dramatic social and political shifts that delivered the Brexit referendum result in 2016, and the general election outcome in 2019.

Is the House of Lords too big?

In recent years, the size of the Lords has prompted criticism. In 2017, the former Commons speaker John Bercow complained that 'it is frankly patently absurd that the House of Lords is significantly larger than the House of Commons' and in 2019 the Electoral Reform Society called the Lords 'grossly over-sized'. Efforts to reduce the size of the Lords have gathered pace in recent years, with the Burns Committee setting out a plan in 2018 to reduce its size to 600.

However, Boris Johnson's dissolution list saw him stand accused of having 'undone years of progress in trying to manage the size of the chamber down', according to Meg Russell of University College London's Constitution Unit. The House of Lords Act 1999 radically reduced the size of the Lords, bringing it almost in line with the Commons. Since then — and in spite of recent debates, votes, inquiries and detailed plans to reduce its size — the size of the Lords has steadily grown to the point at which the second chamber far exceeds the first, and indeed any equivalent democratic state's second chamber.

Table 7.1 Lords appointments from 2000 by prime minister

Prime minister	Years in office	Peerage appointments
Tony Blair	10	374
Gordon Brown	3	34
David Cameron	6	245
Theresa May	3	40

Source: adapted from the House of Lords Library Briefing Paper on life peerages

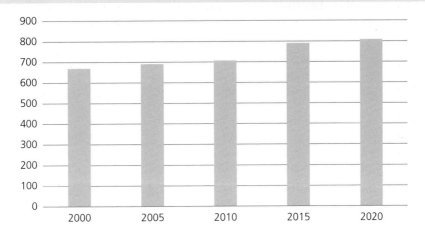

Figure 7.1 Growth in size of the House of Lords, 2000–2020

Source: adapted from figures supplied by the House of Lords Library and House of Lords Information Office

With Theresa May broadly sticking to the planned reduction, only appointing an average of 13 per year over her 3 years in office, Boris Johnson was deemed to have purposely ignored the push for reform in what Lord Fowler, the lord speaker and former Tory cabinet minister, referred to as a 'massive policy U-turn'.

Indeed the sheer size of the Lords is seen by many as undermining its operational efficiency. The Lords is unique among democratic countries in permitting appointments for life with no overall cap on total size. Consequently, according to peers such as Baroness D'Souza, its size now 'interferes with the proper execution of our duties' in limiting time for questions and reducing the chamber's ability and capacity to hold the government to account. In addition to this, the recent growth has also increased the cost — to over £20 million a year in Lords' expenses alone.

Has the House of Lords become too partisan?

One of the trends in recent years is for prime ministers to use their terms of office to rebalance the House of Lords in their party's favour. However, with the Conservatives in power for last 10 years, and with three general elections and three different prime ministers during that time, the opportunities for packing the Lords (via dissolution and resignation lists) have been greater than usual.

Box 7.5	'The way members of our second chamber are chosen casts a pall of corruption over Westminster'

Boris Johnson's latest nominations to the House of Lords are shameless. This is no reflection on the individuals concerned, merely on the decrepit state of the constitution that selects them… It reminds us of a theory constantly denied, but often posed: that membership of the British parliament can effectively be purchased. No British minister should ever… accuse foreign countries of corruption as long as this stain hovers over Westminster's democracy.

Source: Simon Jenkins, 'Boris Johnson's list of lords is a disgrace', *The Guardian*, 3 August 2020

Nine years of appointments by Tony Blair had made the Labour Party by 2006 the largest single party in the Lords. It took the Conservatives until 2015 to surpass them. Since then, while Labour's lead had only ever been marginal, the Conservative lead was substantial even before Boris Johnson's appointments. Statistics include:

- In the 10 years from 2010, the total number of Labour peers has declined from 211 to 179.
- Since 2010, Conservative peers have grown in number from 189 to 261.
- A Labour lead of 22 in 2010 (when the party was last in office with a Commons majority of 66) has become a Conservative lead of 82 (with a Commons majority of 80) in 2020.

While the Burns Committee report emphasised the need for 'balanced appointments' according to 'a clear formula', Boris Johnson's 36 appointments included 19 Conservatives and 5 Labour peers, plus 12 who were either cross-bench or non-affiliated. In the view of Meg Russell: 'Johnson has very plainly flouted this principle, leaving Labour at a major disadvantage, and weakening parliamentary oversight powers as a result.'

Is it time to fully reform the Lords?

The most recent analysis (quoted in the *New Statesman*) indicates that over a 10-month period between 2019 and 2020 the average life peer:

- claimed £20,935 in expenses
- contributed to 12 debates
- produced 7 written questions
- voted 23 times

In addition, 140 failed to take part in any debates, less than half sat on a committee and over 70 voted between 1 and 5 times in total. The expense, size, appointment structure and partisanship of the House of Lords make it ripe for reform in the view of many commentators.

Table 7.2 Is it time to fully reform the Lords?

YES	NO
Following the most recent appointments, the number of peers stands at over 800. Former lord speaker and ex-Conservative minister Lord Fowler complained in the aftermath of Boris Johnson's 36 appointments that 'we have very important duties to carry out in terms of the governance of this country but we don't need 830 to do it'.	The size of the Lords is far less relevant than the capability that it contains. Additionally, the removal of most hereditary peers means that even now, the House is more than 500 peers lower than it was. It is difficult to deny the expertise of many recent additions, particularly those able to contribute to the expanding realms of science, healthcare and technology.
A second chamber need not be wholly elected, thereby set up to tussle for democratic legitimacy with the Commons. Ireland's unelected, senatorial model for a second chamber is often cited as a strong and functional example of a similar alternative.	Unicameral legislatures are rare, and the UK's centralised, executive-dominant system would not benefit from the elimination of a second chamber altogether. However, there has yet to be agreement on an alternative.
2020 highlighted the unregulated appointment process: there are no enforceable constraints on how many peers a PM can appoint to the House of Lords. Although appointments are made by the Queen, convention requires her to act on prime ministerial advice. Prime ministers have routinely used the system to appoint unexceptional allies and friends.	'Cronyism' is a standard argument levelled by political opponents, and one that Labour's Tony Blair was equally charged with. However, Johnson also appointed several well-respected and outspoken former Labour MPs in Gisela Stuart, Kate Hoey, Frank Field, Ian Austin and John Woodcock, though all five are united by their support for Brexit or antipathy towards Jeremy Corbyn.
Criticism remains that the daily attendance rate of £323 is a strong incentive for many to just 'turn up' without making much of a democratic difference. With a Lords' expenses bill already topping £20 million, the Electoral Reform Society estimates that Boris Johnson's new appointments alone will cost the taxpayer an extra £1.1 million in attendance allowances and expenses.	Its power to amend legislation and delay bills by a year is important. Despite urging reform, Simon Jenkins in *The Guardian* refers to it as a 'welcome theatre in which the voice of age and experience is not drowned out by the mass media's obsession with youth'. Recent debates on Article 50 and the Withdrawal Bill saw the expertise and measured prudence of the Lords widely praised.

Connections and comparisons

- Comparing second chambers does not play out well for the UK's House of Lords. Second chambers in France, Italy and Germany — whose first chambers are similar in size to the House of Commons — comprise 348, 320 and 69 members respectively. The Chinese People's Congress, which operates more as an annual conference than a permanent assembly, is the only second chamber in the world that is larger than the House of Lords.
- The House of Lords is not just generally unrepresentative, it is specifically so. Up to 1958, the Lords was an all-male chamber. Following the Life Peerages Act an increasing number of women have been appointed. The first female member was Irene Curzon, whose father had led the opposition to women's suffrage in 1914. Since 1958 though, of the nearly 1,500 life peers appointed, less than a quarter (21%) have been women. Before Boris Johnson's 2020 nominations there were 773 peers, 212 of whom were women. While just over a quarter of Conservative peers are female, the figures are 39% for Labour and 36% for the Liberal Democrats. In Boris Johnson's list of 36, just one third were women.

Exam success

The *Daily Mirror* recently described the House of Lords as 'an outdated, anarchic, unrepresentative institution we'd be lost without'. However, Walter Bagehot also commented that as long ago as the late nineteenth century 'the cure for admiring the House of Lords is to go and look at it'. It would be fair to say that while a lot of attention is paid to the unelected and unrepresentative nature of the House of Lords, a more appropriate alternative has yet to receive a consensus. Examination questions on the House of Lords could be structured as follows:

- Evaluate the extent to which the House of Lords should be reformed in favour of a fully elected alternative. (Edexcel-style, 30 marks)
- 'The House of Lords should be reformed in favour of a fully elected alternative.' Analyse and evaluate this statement. (AQA-style, 25 marks)

The best responses will evaluate the strengths and weaknesses of the various approaches to constructing an alternative second chamber — fully appointed, fully elected, or a mixture of both. In addition, attention would need to be given to the fact that a chamber with greater democratic legitimacy might well demand increased powers — such as the ability to veto, not just delay, legislation.

What next?

Research: 'Boris Johnson's 36 new peerages make the need to constrain prime ministerial appointments to the House of Lords clearer than ever', Meg Russell, 31 July 2020, The Constitution Unit, **https://constitution-unit.com**

Read: the House of Lords Library Briefing Paper, 'Life Peerages Created Since 1958', 11 October 2018, **https://lordslibrary.parliament.uk**

Chapter 8

Parliament and the executive: the impact of the health crisis on their relationship

Focus

The relationship between Parliament and the executive is a prominent feature of all examination specifications, not to mention the subject of intense scrutiny and debate more widely. Students need to be able to evaluate the effectiveness of all the various ways that Parliament can hold the executive to account and in particular demonstrate an understanding of the changing balance of power between Parliament and the executive.

Edexcel	UK Government 2.4, 4.2	The way in which Parliament interacts with the executive and the relationship between the executive and Parliament
AQA	3.1.1.2	Scrutiny of the executive and the interaction of Parliament with other branches of government

Context

Just as were so many other areas of social and political life, the relationship between Parliament and the executive was transformed by the measures put in place to control the transmission of the coronavirus. As noted by many commentators, parliamentary scrutiny is a vital cornerstone of the UK's parliamentary system — never more needed at a time of national crisis, such as against the backdrop of an unfolding health crisis, but much harder to perform.

The UK Parliament is similar to many legislatures across the world in that systems and procedures are based almost entirely on the physical presence of legislator–representatives in the assembly building. However, lockdown and social distancing rules meant that from mid-April onwards, processes over the course of 2020 — such as parliamentary questions, ministerial statements, select committee hearings and legislative proceedings, in the Commons and Lords — were conducted either wholly or partly in 'virtual' form.

It would be surprising if the work of Parliament had not been substantially degraded by these changes. Of particular note were the reduction in quality and spontaneity of parliamentary debates and the lack of opportunities for representatives to speak to ministers in the division lobbies. Even after the return to the Commons, questions were raised as to whether — with so many restrictions and exclusions — a partial resumption of parliamentary activity, as opposed to a 'full' but virtual resumption, was a compromise too far.

However, students of politics require contemporary examples of both the effectiveness of parliamentary scrutiny and the changing balance of power between the branches, made especially relevant during the course of the health crisis. While scrutiny also takes place in the House of Lords, the main focus in 2020 includes the activities and work of:

- backbenchers in the House of Commons
- select committee scrutiny, inquiries and reports
- the leader of the opposition at Prime Minister's Questions

Box 8.1 Key definitions

Parliamentary scrutiny: the investigation, examination and analysis of government policies, actions and spending. It is carried out by representatives in the House of Commons, on behalf of their constituents, and in the House of Lords and takes place in the chambers and committees.

The executive: the branch of government that executes and administers laws passed by the legislature. In the UK, the executive is made up of the prime minister, cabinet, government ministers and senior civil servants within the departments of state.

Backbenchers: MPs who do not hold office within government and therefore do not sit on the front benches of the Commons chamber. The threat of 'backbench rebellions' when governments hold slender Commons majorities is a source of instability and insecurity for many prime ministers.

The role of backbenchers during the health crisis

In 2020 the mood of government backbenchers in the Commons was far less restless than in recent years as the substantial Commons majority secured by Boris Johnson following the 2019 general election had ended almost a decade of narrow or non-existent governing majorities. The health crisis played a substantial part in the relative composure of the Commons, especially with the restricted nature of social interaction, and the acceptance among Tory backbenchers that support for the government during the crisis was close to mandatory.

However, as recent years have demonstrated, even in a crisis, backbench support can never entirely be relied upon, and there were several stand-offs resulting in government concessions to avoid full-blown backbench rebellions.

- Cooperation was needed to avert a backbench rebellion over plans to override part of the terms of the EU divorce treaty, a move which would have seen the UK breaking international law. In September 2020, when up to 30 Conservative MPs abstained in a vote following the UK Internal Market Bill's first reading, the government compromised with an amendment that made parliamentary agreements necessary prior to any move by the government to breach the EU divorce treaty.
- In late September 2020, threats by 'more than 80 Conservative MPs', according to *The Guardian*, over the government's renewal of coronavirus legislation led to several concessions by the government to avert a backbench rebellion, including that MPs would get to vote on new lockdown measures — such as the 'rule of six'.

The debate and vote to extend the measures of the Coronavirus Act took place in late September 2020, with 330 MPs voting in favour, 24 against and 300 abstaining.

The work of select committees

The Commons Liaison Committee scrutinises the prime minister, May 2020

The committee that comprises the chairs of all select committees was finally set up in May 2020 following a departure from established practice — instead of the committee selecting its own chair, the government installed Sir Bernard Jenkin. Boris Johnson's early remote appearance before the committee was, according to Hannah White, deputy director of the Institute for Government, 'notable for the gaps in his knowledge and lack of preparation'.

Box 8.3 **Select committees**

Parliamentary committees set up to scrutinise the policy and practice of the executive are known as select committees. They are split between departmental select committees (those that scrutinise the work of one area of government such as the Defence Committee) and non-departmental select committees (such as the Public Accounts Committee or the Backbench Business Committee), which have much wider briefs.

Committees demonstrate their value when chairs focus questions on their respective policy areas. In this instance:

- Jeremy Hunt, chair of the Health and Social Care Committee and former secretary of state for health, extracted an admission from the prime minister that the UK had not learnt the lessons of SARS or MERS, and that Public Health England did not have the appropriate capacity, testing kits or laboratory staff as the pandemic unfolded.
- Greg Clark, chair of the Science and Technology Committee, questioned the deficiencies of the government's test and trace policy, and highlighted the disparity between the UK's social distancing guideline of 2 metres, which was greater than most other countries' 1 or 1.5 metre rules. Commentators noted

the prime minister's apparent lack of clarity and detail in his responses, though he promised to 'look again at the issues'.

In mid-June, and within 4 weeks of the prime minister's liaison committee appearance, the UK government reduced its 2-metre social distancing rule.

The Health and Social Care Select Committee reports on care services during the pandemic

Select committees in the House of Commons also conduct inquiries and produce thorough reports in their respective policy areas. The reports are designed to review existing practice, highlight deficiencies and make detailed recommendations to the government in light of the evidence gathered.

In early October 2020 the Health and Social Care Select Committee produced a report that sought to 'assess the impact and unprecedented challenge caused by COVID-19 to the provision of essential services' by focusing on key aspects of health and social care services particularly affected by the pandemic. These included such things as waiting times and appointment backlogs, the availability of PPE and routine testing for NHS and care staff, staff stress and burnout, and lessons learnt for the future to support the NHS.

The committee heard evidence from cancer patients who confirmed that they had been left in limbo, 'sitting at home knowing that all the cancers are growing [with] absolutely no word at all from the hospital about when some treatment might start'. It examined details relating to the confusion over shielding guidance, and the dire consequences of the postponement of surgical operations. It also listened to testimony on the disruption to and extra demands on mental health services from figures such as chief executive of NHS England, Sir Simon Stevens, on the disruption to and extra demands on mental health services, and from NHS and care staff at significant risk due to fatigue and exhaustion.

Recommendations of the report were wide-ranging, but specific, many with deadlines. For example:

- On waiting times: 'we ask the Department of Health and Social Care and NHS England for an update on what steps are being taken and what steps will be taken in the future to manage the overall level of demand across health services, by the end of October 2020'.
- On protective equipment: 'we ask the Department of Health and Social Care to update us by the end of November 2020 on how they will ensure a consistent and reliable supply of appropriately fitting PPE to all NHS staff in advance of the start of winter and a potential second wave'.

The leader of the opposition and prime minister's questions

Prime Minister's Questions (PMQs) provides a weekly opportunity for the leader of the opposition to raise issues and to question the prime minister when the House is in session.

Over the course of 2020, and since installed as leader of the opposition, Sir Keir Starmer used the opportunity to 'prosecute an argument that the Prime Minister is incompetent, insufficiently on top of the detail and leading a failing government' (Ailbhe Rea, *New Statesman*, September 2020).

- In June 2020, the leader of the opposition focused on deficiencies in the UK's track and trace system. Keir Starmer reminded the prime minister that he had 'promised a world-beating system would be in place by 1 June'. However, Starmer raised the fact that in early June more than two thirds of those who should have been contacted, had not been, suggesting this was a 'big problem'.
- In July 2020, Keir Starmer attacked Boris Johnson's 'flippant' attitude to the relaxation of lockdown rules that had resulted in a 'major incident' on Bournemouth beach. He also accused the prime minister of being 'so slow to act' regarding the rise in coronavirus cases in Leicester, which had led to a localised lockdown.
- In September 2020, the leader of the opposition used PMQs to challenge the prime minister on the support for workers, stating that Boris Johnson 'just doesn't get it' on the severe threat to many people's jobs and on new lockdown regulations: '… if the prime minister doesn't understand the rules, how does he expect the rest of the country to understand and follow the rules?'

The format of PMQs is often criticised, leading to accusations that in the era of 24-hour news, the internet and social media, leaders are searching for opportunities to insert their pre-prepared quips and soundbites, ones that can be clipped and shared, usually out of context, on various media platforms. In addition, the odds are stacked in favour of a prime minister, who always has the last word.

These two features together can lead to some odd exchanges. For example, on 30 September 2020, instead of the leader of the opposition using all six questions to focus on the government's handling of the health crisis, he used five and finished with a change of tack for his sixth and final question — asking about Black History Month and the disproportionate deaths in pregnancy and childbirth among black women in the UK. A wrong-footed prime minister briefly explained his intention for a 'full review', before delivering his pre-prepared finale to a health-related question that had never been asked.

Connections and comparisons

- While the US Congress is based to a greater or lesser extent on the working of the British Parliament, the two institutions have developed and evolved in very different directions over several centuries. The 'little legislatures' of the US Congress wield significant power in what prompted Woodrow Wilson to write that 'it is not far from the truth to say that Congress in session is Congress on public exhibition, whilst Congress in its committee rooms is Congress at work'.

■ The growing autonomy of congressional committees coupled with the polarisation and fragmentation of the congressional chambers is often said to have weakened Congress in relation to the executive and judiciary. However, it is the investigations and reports by congressional committees that have often laid the foundations for some of the biggest developments, and indeed 'moments' — such as when the Senate Judiciary Committee rejects a president's Supreme Court nominee — in US political history.

Exam success

Students should be clear on all the ways that Parliament can scrutinise the executive and how effective that scrutiny is. In addition the best answers to essay questions on this topic will communicate that the balance of power between the two branches is constantly changing. Essay questions may be framed as follows:

■ Evaluate the argument that Parliament is ineffective in checking the power of the executive. (Edexcel-style, 30 marks)
■ 'Parliament is ineffective in checking the power of the executive.' Analyse and evaluate this statement. (AQA-style, 25 marks)

With contemporary examples in mind, students should also look to include wider constitutional issues and arrangements. In the UK, an uncodified constitution, a majoritarian electoral system (which has often handed governments substantial majorities), and a lack of separation of powers has meant that the executive retains dominance over the legislature.

What next?

Read: Dr Alice Lilly and Dr Hannah White, 'Parliament's role in the coronavirus crisis: holding the government to account', 21 May 2020, Institute for Government, www.instituteforgovernment.org.uk

Read: 'The return of the Liaison Committee has added to the prime minister's coronavirus problems' by Hannah White of the Institute for Government, 28 May 2020, www.instituteforgovernment.org.uk

Read: 'How can core NHS and care services be supported during the pandemic and beyond?' by MPs on the Health and Social Care Select Committee, October 2020, https://houseofcommons.shorthandstories.com

Chapter 9

The prime minister: how effective was Boris Johnson in controlling the health crisis?

Focus

The nature and scope of prime ministerial power, including relations with the cabinet and the wider executive, feature in all examination specifications. As well as studying sources of and restraints on prime ministerial power, students are required to study the influence of at least two prime ministers in detail, one from the period between 1945 and 1997 and one from the post-1997 period, to illustrate the effectiveness of prime ministers in dictating events and determining policy.

Edexcel	UK Government 3.3	The powers of the prime minister and the cabinet to dictate events and determine policy
AQA	3.1.1.3	The power of the prime minister and cabinet to dictate events and determine policy

Context

The health crisis of 2020 was an exceptional and rapidly evolving phenomenon requiring governments across the globe to grapple with circumstances and challenges the likes of which they had rarely, if ever, encountered before. Like other global leaders, the UK prime minister was thrust into the unwelcome role of controlling a global pandemic. Boris Johnson's subsequent handling of the health crisis has prompted intense debate and offers a valuable contemporary case study in the effectiveness of prime ministers in dictating events and determining policy.

The UK's uncodified arrangements, and the lack of precision and clarity around the role of the prime minister and the relationship between the executive and Parliament, makes evaluating any prime minister's effectiveness all the more challenging.

Prime ministerial power includes:

■ the ability to appoint and dismiss ministers, manage cabinet meetings and structure government departments
■ leading and managing the parliamentary party as the leader of the largest party in the House of Commons
■ providing national leadership, especially in times of crisis, and representing the UK's interests on the global stage

> However, factors that can have a variable influence on the power and influence of the prime minister include:
>
> - the size of a prime minister's governing majority in the Commons
> - the unity of the cabinet and the authority of a prime minister over his or her executive and government
> - leadership style, personality and charisma
> - the impact of 'events', circumstances and issues beyond a prime minister's immediate control

In what ways was the prime minister effective in dictating events during the health crisis?

The *Financial Times* reported in March 2020, before the introduction of national lockdown measures, that 'whatever reservations some people have about Boris Johnson, they recognise the exceptional nature of the coronavirus emergency and understand that there will be mistakes in addressing it'.

Indeed a full and accurate evaluation — one that considers the varied approaches taken by different governments adopting different control measures, different testing regimes and calculations for cases and death rates, each supported by different levels of national healthcare provision — may never be entirely possible.

Initial support for Boris Johnson's leadership was strong

Boris Johnson's brand of leadership, often described as one of 'breezy optimism', appeared to be appreciated in the early days of the virus. In mid-March 2020 — following fewer than 150 deaths related to Covid-19 — the prime minister's approach remained entertaining and defiant. Johnson asserted that while 'often accused of being unnecessarily boosterish about things', within 12 weeks Britain could 'send coronavirus packing' if government guidelines were stuck to.

Four days later, over 25 million viewers watched Boris Johnson's first national address, during which full national lockdown measures were announced. Several weeks later in mid-April, over 66% of respondents to a YouGov survey said that Boris Johnson was doing 'well' as prime minister, with just 26% of respondents saying that they thought he was doing 'badly'.

In addition, as discussed in Chapter 1, there was widespread support for the imposition of lockdown measures with 89% of respondents to an Ipsos MORI poll in the early days of April 2020 saying that they strongly (68%) or tended to (21%) support the measures. Many were reassured by the prime minister's attempts to ensure that political decisions were based upon scientific evidence.

It was not until early June 2020 that Boris Johnson's net approval rating became negative, reasons for which appear later in this chapter.

The government's economic measures were widely supported

In March 2020 the chancellor, Rishi Sunak, said that the government was prepared to do 'whatever it takes' to tackle the financial and economic fallout from the coronavirus. Announcement of an unprecedented economic stimulus package, guaranteed loan systems, increased grants and rate relief were widely supported as many millions feared for their livelihoods.

Box 9.1 **'Support measures are substantial'**

Chancellor Rishi Sunak is also rising to the challenge. His £350bn support package to the economy this week put meat on his 'whatever it takes' promise to support business and the economy. The pledge on Friday that all companies — including non-profit enterprises — can claim grants of 80 per cent of salaries for furloughed workers, up to £2,500 a month, is a bold and substantial one.

Source: 'UK government is finally coming to grips with coronavirus',
Financial Times, 20 March 2020

Six months later in mid-September 2020, almost 3 million workers (12% of the UK's workforce) remained on partial or full furlough leave — government support for as much as 80% of a monthly wage up to a maximum of £2,500. The 'job support scheme' replaced the furlough scheme in the autumn of 2020, and saw the government subsidising the pay of employees working fewer than normal hours due to lower demand. In all a total of 9.4 million jobs were furloughed at some point in 2020.

The economic measures, in particular the job support scheme, were not without their critics. In September 2020, shadow chancellor Anneliese Dodds accused the chancellor of 'pulling up the drawbridge' on workers by 'forcing employers to choose which staff to keep and which to fire'. But official figures provided by HM Treasury in September 2020 showed that the furlough scheme had saved many millions of jobs, with the majority of them (from 30% of the workforce down to 11% by May) moving back into work over the summer.

The UK led the way in identifying and developing treatments

With substantial backing and support from the prime minister and government, the UK was at the forefront of medical developments during the health crisis.

- By August 2020 over 100,000 people had signed up for government-backed Covid-19 vaccine trials, overseen by the government's vaccines taskforce.
- In September 2020, the prime minister announced the UK government's pledge of £500 million towards a new global vaccine-sharing scheme to ensure the fair sharing of treatments for Covid-19.

In June 2020, the UK's national clinical trial to explore different treatments for those hospitalised established that the low-cost steroid dexamethasone could reduce death by up to a third in patients with severe respiratory complications. It was a breakthrough treatment that was adopted worldwide, contrasting markedly with US president Donald Trump's championing of hydroxychloroquine, which British laboratories conclusively proved to have no beneficial effects.

In addition, it was British laboratories and pharmaceutical companies that led the way in 2020 with their investigations into the use of antibiotics, anti-inflammatory and convalescence treatments to tackle the worst symptoms of the virus. And the UK's University of Oxford/AstraZeneca team was among the frontrunners in the development of an effective vaccine.

Effective management of the 'second wave'

In the autumn of 2020, the much-anticipated second wave of confirmed cases far surpassed that of the first. That said:

- By mid-November, the rise in daily hospital admissions flattened at under 1,500 — well below the admissions peak of the previous April.
- At the height of testing, more than 2 million tests were processed over a 7-day period in early November.
- The measures introduced, such as the tiered system, which responded to case variances in different areas, the 'rule of 6' (the maximum number permitted to meet) and the November lockdown were ultimately seen to have contributed to the effective management of the spread of the virus.

While Boris Johnson was widely condemned for the government's handling of the health crisis, cases in Germany peaked at very similar levels to the UK in November 2020, and daily confirmed cases in France, Spain, Italy and many other densely populated European countries (in spite of under half the number of tests being processed in many of them) far surpassed the UK during the 'second wave' in late 2020.

In what ways did the prime minister fail to control events effectively?

Even the staunchest supporters of Boris Johnson found unequivocal praise for his government's handling of the health crisis difficult to sustain. As the crisis unfolded, sympathetic commentaries became increasingly characterised by attempts to draw a line under past mistakes and to urge a new and more coherent approach.

Box 9.2 How Boris can get Britain's Covid fight back on track

It's hard to deny that Boris Johnson's government has so far had a 'bad war' against the pandemic. Our death toll is high compared to other countries and our economy is in worse shape. We face rising cases, increased hospital admissions and more restrictions. It's all so bleak; yet that is why now is precisely the moment for Boris to imitate his great hero, Winston Churchill.

Source: Richard Dobbs, 'A Churchillian task', *The Spectator,* 26 September 2020

Perhaps one of the most marked features over the course of crisis was the steady decline in trust in Boris Johnson and his government.

Box 9.3 **Trust**

Trust is an essential element of the relationship between government and governed in liberal democracies, and a prerequisite upon which governments base their authority. However, declining levels of trust in politicians is a long-standing trend of most modern democratic states.

Many factors, a lot of them unique to the UK's experience and its handling of the crisis, provide evidence of the ineffectiveness of the prime minister and government in controlling events and determining policy during the health crisis.

- **The timing of the lockdown.** Some members of the Scientific Advisory Group for Emergencies (SAGE) argued that the government imposed the lockdown too late, and at the cost of many lives. The lack of early robust data — a total of just 1,215 people had been tested by 11 March 2020 (see information on testing rates below) — coupled with the unwillingness of the government to engage with the severity of the impending crisis, made a timelier decision very difficult.
- **Modelling by Imperial College London.** Among others, Lord Sumption highlighted the way that the government was forced into lockdown on 23 March by a report from former government advisor Neil Ferguson. The epidemiologist was nicknamed 'Professor Lockdown' for his modelling that predicted 510,000 coronavirus deaths in the 'worst-case scenario' — and that lockdown would only work if it was kept in place until there was a vaccine. Professor Ferguson quit his role on SAGE in May after admitting to breaking his own lockdown rules.
- **The supply of personal protective equipment (PPE).** There was widespread criticism of the government's failure to buy and stockpile crucial protective equipment, against the advice of its own advisory body on pandemics, the New and Emerging Respiratory Virus Threats Advisory Group (Nervtag). In the early weeks of the pandemic, senior NHS staff reported that staff lives were being put at risk because of the shortage of PPE.
- **Testing rates.** The centralisation of testing laboratories within the NHS over many years has steadily improved reliability and consistency. However, it has left the UK without the levels of private suppliers that operate in other countries to swiftly expand the production of testing capacity. While the UK may be a world leader in diagnostics, it lacked the ability to produce testing kits to the scale required early in the crisis, only just reaching 10,000 a day in early April 2020, partly impacted by the government's inexplicable decision to briefly halt its testing in March.
- **Levels of infections and deaths.** The lateness into lockdown, the lack of PPE and the failure to instigate large-scale testing sooner led to far higher rates of infection and deaths than other similar countries. However, while some measurements (such as the number of excess deaths per million of the

population) place the UK substantially higher than most, analysis needs to factor in huge variances in testing rates and the comparable accuracy of submitted figures.

- **The Dominic Cummings row.** Dominic Cummings, the prime minister's chief advisor, made a journey from London to Durham and back during the lockdown. Opinion was divided as to whether Cummings had breached statutory regulations (those enforceable by the police) or government-issued guidance, or had simply followed his own instincts in acting reasonably to look after his family in very difficult personal circumstances. Cummings remained in office, yet a poll commissioned by the *Daily Mail* in May 2020 indicated that almost two-thirds of the public thought he should resign.

- **Local lockdowns.** For many outside London in March, there appeared to be little evidence in their areas to justify the imposition of a highly detrimental national lockdown. Yet when raised infection rates were detected in places other than the capital from June, lockdowns were imposed locally in a way that felt unfair, especially as they appeared to target more deprived areas.

- **Examination grades.** The system for awarding grades in the absence of examinations was widely branded a 'fiasco'. Following the cancellation of examinations, schools were compelled to compile rank orders and apply grades that resembled those of previous years. An algorithm to moderate these grades led to countless individual injustices. However, the government U-turn, which saw school grades returned to, led to a different set of issues related to unstandardised grades.

- **Re-opening schools.** There was widespread criticism of the government's handling of the re-opening of schools from June 2020. In late May, the Department for Education (DfE) guidance changed almost daily, and there was persistent unsettling conflict between the government, teaching unions, councils and school leaders. In the end, only the first phase of re-opening took place, meaning that some children returned to almost normal while many did not return at all. In September, the return of students to university campuses was the source of further significant outbreaks.

- **Track and trace failures.** The digital track and trace programme was the path out of lockdown, yet the NHS Covid-19 app was not available until September 2020 and was beset by problems throughout its roll-out. In August 2020, it was reported that failure rates were as high as 50% and the scheme was costing hundreds of millions.

Box 9.4 Track and trace failure

The government's £10bn contact-tracing programme failed to reach almost half the contacts named by infected patients in 'non-complex' cases — including people living under the same roof. The outsourcing giants Serco and Sitel are being paid £192m to provide 18,500 call handlers who are responsible for tracing non-complex contacts referred to them.

Source: 'Coronavirus: track and trace fails in 50% of "easiest" cases', *Sunday Times*, 2 August 2020

- **The November lockdown.** After emphatic pledges from the prime minister and senior government ministers that a second lockdown would not be imposed, the government announced new national restrictions from 5 November 2020. For many, it was just the latest in a sequence of U-turns, and yet more evidence of government ineffectiveness and incompetence.

Connections and comparisons

- Global Citizen, a group that seeks to provide information on global challenges, revealed the countries that had emerged as 'pioneers in epidemic response and virus containment efforts' during the health crisis:
  - New Zealand took 'first place' for its Covid-19 response, according to the Global Response Index. Taking measures within 3 days of the World Health Organization's (WHO) warnings of a public health emergency in January 2020, the country had reported just 1,914 cases and 25 deaths 10 months later.
  - Senegal, despite having a far less sophisticated health care system, took 'second place' with under 15,484 cases and 321 deaths over the same 10-month period. Senegal's development and implementation of contingency and mitigation plans as early as January 2020 were widely praised as having saved many lives.
- In May 2020, Jonathan Freedland in *The Guardian* reported that 'the only thing protecting the prime minister from harsher criticism of his failures is that the US president's are even worse'. The executive response to the health crisis in the USA is widely considered to be bizarre at best. Comments about injecting bleach, conspiracy theories about the virus emerging from Wuhan laboratories, derision for those wearing masks and the president's own hospitalisation with the virus were part of a national response that were accompanied by far higher case and death rates, by almost any measure, than anywhere else in the world.

Exam success

Examination questions on this topic will require students to balance the evidence of control and influence that relate to Boris Johnson's handling of the health crisis with other prime ministers' effectiveness. Questions may be framed as follows:

- Evaluate the argument that UK prime ministers have significant power to dictate events and determine policy. (Edexcel-style, 30 marks)
- 'The UK prime minister's power to dictate events and determine policy is shaped mainly by events outside their control.' Analyse and evaluate this statement. (AQA-style, 25 marks)

Other case studies and examples to support high level responses may include Margaret Thatcher's attempts to introduce the poll tax in 1990, John Major's handling of Conservative Party division over EU membership in the mid-1990s, Tony Blair's invasion of Iraq in 2003, David Cameron's management of the EU referendum process in 2016, and Theresa May's approach to Brexit up to 2019.

What next?

Watch: Boris Johnson's address to the nation announcing the easing of lockdown in May 2020: **www.youtube.com/watch?v=CtQ7osi32jk**

Read: 'Five countries that are getting COVID-19 responses right' by Sophie Partridge-Hicks, 11 September 2020, **www.globalcitizen.org**